And as Jesus passed forth from there he saw a man named Matthew sitting at the receipt of custom and he saith unto him "follow me" and he arose and followed him. And it came to pass as Jesus sat at meat in the house behold many publicans and sinners came and sat down with him and his disciples. And when the Pharisees saw it they said unto his disciples "Why does your Master eat with publicans and sinners?" But when Jesus heard that he said to them "They that are whole need not a physician but only they that are sick."

Gospel of St. Matthew 9:9-11. King James Version
Copyright © 1990 Thomas Nelson Inc.

The Diaries of St. Matthew

A drama based on his Gospel

MANO GOVINDARAJ

WestBow
PRESS
A DIVISION OF THOMAS NELSON

By the same author...

1. **The Matriverse & Other Essays** © 2010.
   (This is a collection of seven essays. The first essay, "The Matriverse" is a hypothesis on the origin of the Universe.

2. **The authorized biography of Jesus Christ—A new interpretation of the Gospel of St. Matthew** © 2012
   (This book presents evidence that most of the Gospel of St. Matthew must have been written during the lifetime of Jesus Christ and its contents were authorized by Him).

WestBow Press books may be ordered through booksellers or by contacting:

WestBow Press
A Division of Thomas Nelson
1663 Liberty Drive
Bloomington, IN 47403
www.westbowpress.com
1 (866) 928-1240

ISBN: 978-1-4908-1256-4 (sc)
ISBN: 978-1-4908-1257-1 (e)

Library of Congress Control Number: 2013918636

Printed in the United States of America.

WestBow Press rev. date: 11/18/2013

THE STRUCTURE OF THE DRAMA

PREFACE

One day Jesus Christ was going past the Roman Tax Office in Capernaum when he saw a young tax official named Matthew at work. Jesus walked up to him and said "Follow me." Matthew did so. Their first conversation evoked such joy in Matthew that he threw a fest in honor of Jesus that very same day in his own house, to which he invited his entire community. Thus a special relationship arose between the two of them immediately.

Writing diaries was a common practice in the ancient world. Taxation involves a great deal of record keeping. Thus Matthew was well trained in keeping records before Jesus called him.

The events of the first eight chapters of the Gospel of St. Matthew happened before Jesus called Matthew. Therefore they are "hearsay" in the hands of Matthew. Who or what was the "source of data" from which Matthew wrote them? From whom did Matthew hear about the marriage of Joseph to the pregnant Mary? Why did Matthew write a glorious eulogy about Joseph in the very first diary? The best explanation is that Jesus told Matthew of his admiration for his earthly father Joseph and Matthew wrote it faithfully.

From a social point of view, it is most unlikely that the "orthodox Jewish" disciples treated Matthew genuinely as an equal. The Diaries end abruptly a few days after the crucifixion; they do not record the appearances of Jesus in the Disciples' lodgings in Jerusalem; they do not record the Ascension of Jesus to Heaven. If the Gospel of Matthew had been written any time afterwards, the writer could not have ended it without the Ascension which became the most significant fact about Jesus to the Sect of the Nazarenes, and was preached to new converts ever afterwards.

The events recorded in the Gospel of St. Mathew have an orderly arrangement very much like a diary. They contain a great deal of drama. Each miracle performed by Jesus was dramatic by itself. Pontius Pilate the Roman Governor was about to start the trial of Jesus when he receives a message from his wife to spare Jesus. How did she know about Jesus? Facing a civil disturbance that may ruin his reputation and career in Rome, Pilate saves his conscience by washing his hands with water publicly in Court before signing the crucifixion decree. Finally the greatest mystery of all - why would Roman soldiers compel an innocent bystander named Simon of Cyrene to carry the cross of Jesus, a condemned prisoner, contrary to Roman Criminal Law? Perhaps Pilate and his counselors were honoring Jesus as a King by relieving him from the indignity of carrying his own cross, the only matter now left in their hands.

How did these facts come exclusively into the knowledge of Matthew unless he was a witness of them? Finally, how did similar texts appear in the synoptic gospels of Matthew, Mark and Luke?

This Drama is constructed in the belief that those persons who put together the original Christian Bible had examined the facts thoroughly and acted in good faith when they recognized the diaries of the tax collector, Matthew, as a Gospel, and placed the Gospel of St. Matthew as the first book of the New Testament.

Mano Govindaraj
Washington D.C.
April 2013

AN ACKNOWLEDGMENT

I acknowledge with gratitude my debt to:

"ESSENTIALS OF SCREENWRITING"
The Art, Craft and Business of Film and Television Writing,
By: Professor Robert Walker,
Professor and Screenwriting Chairman, UCLA
© 2010

(The reader is sure to enjoy its wit, philosophy,
numbered "Principles", and technical expertise even
if one is not aspiring to enter that profession.)

CONVENTIONS USED
IN THIS DRAMA

1. A new scene is indicated by INT or EXT
    INT means the scene takes place indoors
    EXT means the scene takes place outdoors

2. When a character first appears, his or her name is shown in UPPER
    CASE

3. The page has four columns:
    Directions about the scene begin at Column 1
    (INT and EXT always appear in Column 1)
    The Dialogue begins at Column 2
    Notes within a dialogue begin at Column 3
    Speaker's name is at Column 4 in UPPER CASE

ACT 1

THE KING CALLS
HIS BIOGRAPHER

EXT   ROMAN TAX OFFICE IN CAPERNAUM

It is an open structure, with the roof resting on pillars but no
walls. There are tables and chairs for tax officials and tax payers.
A few soldiers are seen. MATTHEW is interviewing JOKIM, a
tax payer.

MATTHEW
"According to our information, you harvested four
hundred bushels of barley this season."

JOKIM
"No, Sir. This year it was only two hundred bushels.

MATTHEW

"Oh, is that so?"

"Well, I am assessing tax of two hundred denarii on your harvest of two hundred bushels of barley"

(JOKIM brightens up)

And

(Writing on a scroll)

A penalty of four hundred denarii for lying about it."

JOKIM
(Alarmed, and half rising on the bench)

"Oh, No, No, No, Sir; Ple-e-e-ease don't do that. I will give you detailed accounts. You can visit my village and see my fields and barns and inquire from neighbors . . ."

They are distracted by a noisy procession on the street. From the middle of the procession JESUS breaks off, and walks towards the tax office. The crowd becomes silent.

Jesus walks directly toward Matthew's table.

JESUS
(Addressing Matthew)

"Follow me."

Matthew looks around, at his supervisor CAPTAIN ARRETUS who is seated comfortably on a 'couch'; then turns his eyes toward Jokim hesitantly for a second and follows Jesus slowly down the four levels of the tax office.

JESUS

"Matthew, thank you for following me out; I have much to say to you."

MATTHEW

"Yes, Rabbi Speak on. I am listening."

JESUS

"I want to discuss with you at length about the Kingdom of Heaven."

MATTHEW

"Rabbi; I am a tax collector. You Rabbis do not want to enter our homes because we are ritually unclean. But we obey all Jewish rules. My forefathers and I have never eaten pork. If you are prepared to come, we can discuss whatever you want comfortably at my home."

JESUS

"Thank you, Matthew. In my Father's kingdom, there are no tax collectors, clean or unclean. I accept your invitation. Let's go."

MATTHEW

"Rabbi, give me a minute."

Matthew turns around towards the Office Manager. CAPTAIN ARRETUS turns his eyes towards Jesus, then back to Matthew, smiles and holds up his hand in approval. Matthew returns to Jesus and leads the way.

The crowd has melted away, leaving only five disciples and four Pharisees.

The group reaches Matthew's house. They wash their feet and enter.

INT   MATTHEW'S HOME

The newcomers are seated in an outer hall. A domestic servant brings in refreshments. Matthew goes inside and speaks to his household.

MATTHEW

"We must honor this Rabbi. Prepare a good feast. Get five goats. Where is BARUCH?"

BARUCH
(A domestic worker)

"Yes, master, here I am."

MATTHEW

"Baruch, I am giving a feast to honor this Rabbi today. Go and tell my mother to come over and supervise the feast. Tell our household helpers to come quickly and help prepare the food. As you go invite our relatives. Do all this very fast. Then go to my office and tell Captain Arretus, that he is invited to the feast with all the staffs in our office. Then see me."

EXT   REAR GARDEN OF MATTHEW'S HOME

The chief butcher comes up to Salome, Matthew's mother, who is directing preparations.

CHIEF BUTCHER

"Lady, I have slaughtered and skinned five fatted goats. Will that be enough?"

SALOME

"Yes, Daniel; now make sure the cooks get them roasted properly."

A FEMALE DOMESTIC comes up to Salome.

FEMALE DOMESTIC

"Flour has been mixed and kneaded. Shall we start baking?"

SALOME

"Don't rush. The meat will take time. Start baking so they will be warm when the feast begins."

INT   FEASTING HALL OF MATHEW'S HOME

Additional helpers are arriving and Salome is instructing them to arrange seating for the feast.

Guests enter. They are seated. Matthew, his parents and grandparents are at the same table with Jesus.

Jesus' five Disciples and four Pharisees are at the next table.

Matthew's boss Captain Arretus is with his staff of tax collectors at a table further away.

Matthew's relatives are at another table. Several ladies, their heads covered are seated by themselves at the end of the Hall. There is a silence.

JESUS

"Abba, we bless this food in your loving name. Let it be nourishment and pleasure for all of us gathered here. Thank you. Amen."

The feast begins; noisy conversation ensues. Servers are going around with loaves of bread, slices of roasted meat, wine and water.

ELIEZER
(Matthew's Grandfather)

"Rabbi, I am so happy you have visited our grandson. He was always a clever boy. He is a favorite of his Tax Office boss, Captain Arretus, that gentleman over there, seated with all his colleagues."

JESUS

"That's nice to know, sir. I do complement your grandson on his achievements."

ELIAKIM, a Pharisee is speaking to PETER at the next table.

ELIAKIM

"The food is excellent, but looks like you people are violating the laws of our elders, don't you think?"

PETER

"Why do you say that, Rabbi? What laws are we violating?"

ELIAKIM

"Did you not know that according to our laws, going into the house of a tax collector and eating with him could make you unclean too?"

PETER

"So?"

ELIAKIM

"So, why does your Master eat with tax collectors, publicans and sinners who are unclean, outcasts? It could make all of you unclean."

PETER

"Well, maybe our Teacher hopes to set new standards of behavior, to treat all Jews as brothers, indeed all humans as brothers; don't you think that would be a good thing?"

ELIAKIM

"Look sharp, young man. Your whole bunch may get into hot water with our leaders in Jerusalem. All of you may find yourselves declared as unclean."

Peter turns round to Jesus at the next table. Jesus has heard Eliakim. Jesus addresses Eliakim.

JESUS

"People in good health do not need a Doctor, but only those who are sick. I did not come to call the righteous, but sinners to repentance."

Eliakim shrugs.

Matthew's colleagues and Captain Arretus make facial expressions of admiration when Jesus replies Eliakim in this manner.

The feast is over. Guests leave. Matthew's parents and grandparents linger with Jesus and the disciples.

SALOME
(Matthew's Mother)
"Rabbi, we are very happy that you visited our home."

JESUS
"Yes, Lady, thank you for treating us to a feast like this."

SALOME
"Sir, you are a wonderful person. You spoke well with Eliakim, the Pharisee. Rabbi, in all our generations we have never eaten any unclean thing, but the Pharisees persist in calling us unclean, and publicans and outcasts."

JESUS
"All of us are children of Abraham, so, we are children of one father. I say we are all children of one God, my Father. The time is coming, soon, when all such ritual differences between us will vanish."

SALOME
"Thank you, Rabbi. I heard that you are from Galilee."

JESUS
"Yes, I am from Nazareth. My mother's name is Mary. My Father is in heaven and has sent me on a mission to save our people from their sins. I am teaching this to my disciples. Would you like your grandson to join me on this mission?"

SALOME

"Rabbi, you are so kind. We will all bless him if he joins you on a mission to change this cruel society. (Smiling) Only Arretus, the Captain of the Tax Office will be unhappy to lose Matthew, he likes him so much."

JESUS

"Thank you, Lady. With his good nature and understanding he will make a useful disciple."

ELIEZER

"Rabbi, once again let me thank you.

We will leave you alone to discuss whatever you want. God Bless all of you."

JESUS

"Peace be upon you all."

The parents and grandparents stay behind. Matthew leads Jesus and the disciples towards his study

INT   MATTHEW'S STUDY

It is large, with tables and chairs. Scrolls and codices are all around, on tables and shelves. There is a bust of Socrates and a bust of Augustus Caesar.

MATTHEW

"Rabbi, it is evening. We have extra rooms where all of you can stay for the night if you wish."

Jesus turns to the disciples.

ANDREW
(A disciple)

"Rabbi, I have that errand to perform early morning. I need to get back to our place tonight."

JESUS
(Addressing his disciples)

"I understand. All of you may return now, together. I will be with you tomorrow morning."

PETER

"Yes, Master, we will await your return."

EXT   STREET LEADING AWAY FROM MATTHEW'S HOME

The disciples leave. On the way they discuss.

JAMES

"Brothers, do you think Jesus plans to make this tax collector also a disciple?"

PETER

"Looks like it."

JAMES

"How come? Do you think we can treat him as a friend? He is a tax collector, a publican, a sinner and an outcast. What say you?"

PETER

"Jesus knows best. Matthew has a lot of money. Maybe he will finance our mission. Frankly, I don't know Jesus' intentions. Let us just trust Jesus, and follow him."

INT   MATTHEW'S STUDY

Jesus and Matthew are just sitting down.

JESUS

"Matthew, thank you for treating us well. Now, tell me about your education.

MATTHEW

"When I was very young I learned The Law and the Prophets. I memorized everything. The Rabbis were impressed. My granddad was pleased and sent me to his friend, Aurelius in the Decapolis. There I joined a Greek School. It had only one teacher, Philippides but he was good. I read all of Homer, Plato and Aristotle by age seventeen. Then I traveled to Greece. I stayed at a boarding house and attended an advanced school. Life in Athens was exciting. It was there that I learned Latin. Captain Arretus was impressed with my Latin and hired me promptly."

MATTHEW

"Rabbi, while you relax, let me quickly write my diary of today's events."

Matthew opens a codex and writes; then applies ink and wipes the papyrus.

MATTHEW

"There! (Reads) Jesus passed that way and saw me sitting at the tax office. He said 'follow me.' And I got up and followed him."

MATTHEW
"Rabbi, does it sound right?

JESUS
"Yes."

MATTHEW
"Rabbi, while writing it a thought occurred to me about how I can help you in your ministry?"

MATTHEW
"For instance I can write a treatise about your new philosophy. I can make copies too, and we can distribute it. That way you can quickly popularize your new philosophy, don't you think?"

JESUS
(Smiles)
"Thank you Matthew. I have a much, much bigger task in mind for you. How much <u>are</u> you prepared to do for me?"

MATTHEW
"Jesus, Master. As a tax collector I deal with many kinds of people. But you are different from all men. I am prepared to do whatever you want me to do for you."

JESUS
"You observed right. I am the Messiah our nation has been waiting so long for. Do you believe this?

MATTHEW
(Excitedly)

"Yes, Yes. I believe you. Otherwise you could not speak to Eliakim like that. These Pharisees are dangerous."

MATTHEW

"Rabbi, if you wish, I could write a brochure saying that you are the Messiah. But if you distribute it, you might upset the Pharisees. Then they will do some nasty things against you."

JESUS

"Matthew, you understand a great deal. I am the Messiah, the anointed of God, the Christ and King of the Jews. The Jews do not accept it. Their elders cannot understand it. They will kill me for it. Then I will rise from the dead on the third day."

MATTHEW
(Smiling)

"Master, if you rise from the dead, that's the greatest miracle I can think of!"

JESUS

"For that very reason the matters I tell you must not be publicized till I rise from the dead. Matthew, my friend, Can you keep a secret?"

MATTHEW

"Master, I am a tax official. My job IS to keep secrets! You can rely on me. But why **would** you keep it secret?"

JESUS

"That is my Father's will, Matthew. I only do His will. Besides, I am telling the Pharisees that I am the Messiah. My disciples need not do so until I rise from the dead."

MATTHEW
(Seriously)

"Master, are you telling me to write something but to keep it secret till you rise from the dead?"

JESUS

"Yes."

Matthew stands up. He walks towards a flight of wooden stairs near the wall and places his foot on the first stair.

MATTHEW

"Master, do you see that trap door up there? That is a special attic. It's where I keep confidential tax records. I will keep your brochure there—till you rise from the dead. No one will see it or even know about it."

JESUS

"You understand me, Matthew. You are an obedient man. I desire that you be a scribe of all that I tell you. Are you willing to do so?"

MATTHEW

"Yes, master. I will write whatever you want and keep silent about them, as you desire."

JESUS

"You understand well. I bless you, Matthew."

ACT 2

THE FAMILY OF THE KING

INT   **MATTHEW'S STUDY**

The conversation continues

MATTHEW

"Master, a good starting point would be your family history. Do you like to tell me?"

JESUS

"Yes, I will. Do you have access to lists of our Jewish genealogies?"

MATTHEW

"Yes, in our tax office we have the genealogy of everyone, to verify ownership of property and taxes to be levied. Those genealogies are too detailed and quite long."

JESUS

"Yes, they are long. You must summarize them so people can read them easily."

MATTHEW

"Tomorrow I will locate your genealogy. What tribe do you belong to, Master?

JESUS

I am descended from the tribe of Judah, from David the King and from Abraham.

Pause

"My earthly father, Joseph was a carpenter. He told me that he married my mother under unusual, actually miraculous circumstances."

Matthew takes a papyrus and stylus.

MATTHEW

"Yes, Master, I am listening."

(THE NARRATION IS DRAMATIZED.)

EXT   SUNRISE; JOSEPH'S CARPENTRY SHOP;

JOSEPH (The earthly father of Jesus) is getting ready for the day's tasks; a friend arrives.

JOSEPH

"Welcome Elias, my friend. Peace be on you. You are very early. What news?"

ELIAS

"Joseph, my friend, greetings, and Peace be on you."

ELIAS
(Sounding serious)

"Joseph, we have known each other since we were little kids, remember?"

JOSEPH

"Yes; so what?"

ELIAS

"I was at dinner last night at Janiss' place. There was the usual gossip. But there was talk about you, Joseph. So I hurried here to tell you before anyone else and to ask whether you are aware of it. That's all."

JOSEPH

"These people are always gossiping. That is why I rarely join their dinners."

ELIAS

"They were talking and joking about you. That woman Martha, she cannot keep her tongue. 'Joseph is engaged to Mary. But Mary seems to be pregnant already.' I was shocked to hear that, Joseph. They were laughing and joking 'Maybe they have been playing the fool already!'"

JOSEPH

"No, my friend; I have not met with her since my betrothal four months ago. I am surprised myself. She is a good girl, and her parents are respectable people. I will check with them."

ELIAS

"I hope everything is going to be alright. I support you Joseph, my friend. You can depend on me always. Peace be upon you."

Elias leaves. He walks slowly away.

EXT   STREET LEADING TO MARY'S HOUSE

Joseph is on his way there. He reaches Mary's home and is met by ELIAB, Mary's father.

ELIAB
(Embracing Joseph)
"Peace be to you, my son. Welcome.

JOSEPH
"Peace be upon you, uncle. Thank you."

ELIAB
"Here, wash your feet and enter."

ELIAB
"Yes, my son, what brings you to visit us at this early hour? Is there anything special?"

JOSEPH
"Yes, sir; my friend Elias brought me some unbelievable information early morning. Is there any truth in that?"

ELIAB
"In what? Tell me a bit more of what he told you. Do not hesitate. Between us, there is no need to hide anything."

JOSEPH

"Elias said there was a dinner at Janiss' place last night. There was gossip that Mary is already pregnant. I refused to believe it. I have a duty to tell you, and also ask you whether it is true."

ELIAB

This is a great puzzle for us too, my son. She is yet only fifteen years old. She has never been out of our sight at any time. After your engagement she had a vision of an angel and she told us about it. A few days ago her mother noticed signs of pregnancy. We, too, are very puzzled indeed."

JOSEPH

"I have the greatest respect for you, Sir, and for your family. What do you think I should do?"

ELIAB

"I too would like to know a bit more. Shall we inquire whether she has anything to say?"

JOSEPH

"Yes, sir, I have no objection."

Eliab enters the inner home. He speaks to the womenfolk and returns. The young MARY comes to the father's presence accompanied by her mother. The two ladies stand by the door.

ELIAB

"Mary, I love you, my daughter. We have betrothed you to be married to Joseph, here. Today he has heard a rumor that you are seemingly pregnant, and does not know what to think of it. Do you have anything to say about it, my dear?"

MARY

"Yes, father. About three months ago I told all of you about my vision of an Angel. The angel told me that I am blessed of God, that I will have a Son who will be the King forever. I actually talked with the angel. After that vision I do feel uneasy and may be pregnant, and I do not know what I can do about it. Everything is God's will. Blessed be God."

ELIAB

"Thank you, my darling child. You have spoken truly. You can return inside."

Mary and her mother withdraw.

ELIAB

"So Joseph, my daughter has told you the truth. There is nothing we as a family can do about it. It is God's will, I think."

JOSEPH

"Really, I am confused. I need to think about it. Let me leave now. As you know, uncle, our laws are very strict, and require me to publicly disgrace a girl if she is pregnant before marriage."

ELIAB

"I know those laws, son. Peace be unto you. Think about it, ask God for guidance, and act as you think fit. Good bye for now."

He leads Joseph affectionately, out of the house, to the street.

INT　　　　JOSEPH'S HOME

Joseph is seen walking around worried, not engaged in any specific work. Night falls. He gets into bed and falls asleep. He is awakened by hearing his name being called.

ANGEL

"Joseph, Joseph."

Joseph hears the voice. He rubs his eyes and looks around. He sees the angel.

ANGEL

"Joseph, Son of David, do not be afraid to marry Mary your wife. What is conceived in her is of the Holy Spirit. She will bear a Son, and you must name him 'Jesus' because he is the one who will save his people from their sins."

Joseph is speechless. The Angel smiles; after a few moments the angel disappears.

EXT　　　　EARLY MORNING

Joseph is walking hurriedly out of his house. He reaches Mary's home.

INT　　　　MARY'S HOME

Joseph is greeted by Mary's father.

ELIAB
(Embracing Joseph)

"Peace be upon you, Joseph. It's nice to see you so early. What may I do for you?"

JOSEPH

"Peace, my dear Sir. Briefly, I have decided that I should marry Mary as soon as possible, without delay."

ELIAB

"That is good news. The Peace of God be upon both of you, my son. Nevertheless, let us do everything in our customary way. Let me see, we need to inform our relatives, and prepare the feast. Tomorrow is the Sabbath. Do you think the second day of next week is good for you?"

JOSEPH

"It is good. Thank you. I too will inform my family and friends and the officiating priest."

EXT   JOSEPH'S HOUSE

Joseph is seen leading Mary, clothed in her bridal dress, to his house. Joseph's family and friends are welcoming the couple.

<u>DRAMATIZATION ENDS</u>

INT   MATTHEW'S STUDY

Matthew looks up from the papyrus he is writing.

JESUS

"My earthly father Joseph told me that he married my mother contrary to all our Jewish laws and customs, not only because the angel commanded him but he actually loved her and thought she was innocent, although she was pregnant already. He said he also trusted and respected her so much, he did not even touch her till I was born."

MATTHEW

"How fascinating? What a narrative!"

Matthew applies ink to the page. He takes another papyrus.

JESUS

"And, Matthew, my dad told me something even more astonishing. A whole caravan came to visit him in Bethlehem after I was born. I must have been a baby at that time."

THE NARRATION IS DRAMATIZED

EXT   JOSEPH'S HOUSE IN BETHLEHEM;

IT IS NIGHT

There are stars in the sky; for a few seconds a brighter Star is seen just above this house. Three Magi, SOTER, MESECH and KALLINI approach it. Kallini knocks on the door.

JOSEPH
(Opening the door and seeing strangers):
"Welcome Sirs. Peace be upon you. May I ask who or what you are looking for?"

SOTER

"Greetings and peace be upon you. We have come to visit you, and your infant child."

JOSEPH

"I am so surprised. Maybe you have made a mistake. I am not a Bethlehemite. I am Joseph from Nazareth in Galilee and I am here only for the registration. Are you sure you have come to the right place?

SOTER

"Yes, Sir. We have come from a very far country and were guided to your house by a Star. We will tell you about it later. First, let us pay our obeisance to this child."

JOSEPH

"Welcome to my humble little home, Sirs."

The Magi remove their sandals. Joseph conducts them into the hallway. From the outer hallway he enters an inner room alone, speaks to Mary and returns. He then conducts them into the inner room where Mary is with the baby. Mary is surprised. The Magi bow low in an attitude of worship for the child.

SOTER
(To Mary)

"Peace be upon you, Lady;"

(To Joseph)

"This child is special."

MESECH
(To Mary)

"Lady, we have come from a very far country in the East, all the way, to see and worship your Son. Peace be upon him and you."

SOTER

"He is a King, born as a King. We have brought gifts fit for this occasion. These gifts are from the sages and scientists of the East. Please accept them from us."

Mary smiles, in an innocent, puzzled way.

SOTER
Opens a box, and shows it to the
child. He bows, and rises.

"Here is a gift of gold. It is fitting for you as a King."

He closes the box and places it in the hands of Joseph.

MESECH
(Bowing low)

"Here is a gift of frankincense. It symbolizes that the whole world will worship you in holiness."

He closes, and hands the box to Joseph.

KALLINI
(Bowing low)

"Here is a gift of myrrh. This gift symbolizes how you will end your ministry on earth."

He closes and hands the box to Joseph.

SOTER
(To Mary)

"My child, you do not know what we have gifted to your infant son. But you will understand later on. Now, the Peace of Almighty God be with all three of you."

MARY

"Thank you, sirs; and go in peace"

The Magi are leaving. They beckon to Joseph to follow them. He closes the door and follows.

ACT 3

THE TALE OF THE SAGES & SCIENTISTS

EXT   **THE MAGI LEAD JOSEPH OUTSIDE**

Joseph sees a parked caravan; there are horses, camels, donkeys and people resting in the fields near his house.

SOTER

"Joseph, you need to know who we are and about our journey. We started about two years ago, when this star appeared. It guided us first to Jerusalem. We thought, perhaps, this child is born in the King's Palace."

THEIR NARRATION IS DRAMATIZED

EXT   CITY OF JERUSALEM EVENING

A caravan arrives and parks in an empty space in Jerusalem. Four Jerusalemites approach the caravan. One of them speaks to people in the caravan.

JERUSALEMITE

"People, where are you coming from?"

A CARAVAN TRAVELER

We are coming from the East, from beyond Susa."

JERUSALEMITE

"So, where are you going?"

CARAVAN TRAVELER

"Only our Caravan Commander knows that. Let me fetch him for you."

He returns with the Commander.

COMMANDER

"Yes, Sirs, someone wanted to know where we are headed? You? I am leading a group of Scientists who want to see your new-born prince. Do you know about your new prince?"

JERUSALEMITE

"Actually, Sir, you must ask that from our King, Herod the Great. Maybe he will visit you. Just be careful of Herod, that's all."

COMMANDER

"Can you show us his Palace?"

ALL FOUR JERUSALEMITES

"Yes."

They lead the commander to Herod's Palace. Night is falling.

INT NEXT DAY; AUDIENCE HALL OF HEROD THE GREAT

Two High Priests, Ten Sadducees, ten Pharisees and ten "elders" are seated in rows. Trumpets sound. Herod arrives and ascends his Throne.

HEROD

"Peace be to you. Welcome, leaders and guides of the people."

GATHERING

"Peace be to you and Welcome. Long live the King."

HEROD

"Thank you and I wish you all well. I believe you are all happy and in good health."

HIGH PRIEST

"Yes, your majesty. We are all well and waiting to perform your commands."

HEROD

"Yes. All of you have heard about these visitors who arrived in Jerusalem yesterday?"

General murmur of acknowledgment is heard.

HEROD

"These visitors have come from the East. They have come with letters from their Emperor. They want to see and pay obeisance to a new-born king of the Jews."

A rustling sound of surprise is heard in the chamber. Herod looks round the Hall, fear and hatred is written on his face.

HEROD

Now, why didn't even one of you tell me about your new-born King?"

Silence

HEROD

"So, tell me now. Where is this new born king? Where is he born?

Soldiers are seen moving around the hall.

HEROD

"I guess none of you will be leaving this Hall, till you reveal to me where your King is born. Is your King born here in Jerusalem or elsewhere?"

HIGH PRIEST

"Your majesty! We have been debating that question every day for over five hundred years. Our Chief Scribe, who keeps the ancient scrolls, will explain this to you, your majesty."

CHIEF SCRIBE

"Long live, O Great King. According to our prophecy Israel's King <u>must</u> be born in Bethlehem. For thus says the prophet—'and you Bethlehem in the land of Judah are not the least among the princes of Judah for out of you shall come forth a Governor that shall rule my people Israel.'"

All those present shake their heads in concurrence.

HEROD
(Addressing the HIGH Priest)
"Chief, do you agree and confirm this revelation by the Chief Scribe?"

HIGH PRIEST
"Yes, your majesty, that is correct."

HEROD
"Thank you. This assembly is ended."

EXT   OUTSIDE THE AUDIENCE HALL

The priests and elders are seen rushing out of several doors of the audience hall.

INT   THE AUDIENCE HALL IS EMPTY. HEROD BECKONS TO A SOLDIER.

HEROD
"Set your guards so that no one can enter this building. Then conduct those visitors to conference Room Number seven."

Herod rises and walks past several rooms to a small chamber deep inside the Hall. The soldier arrives, leading three Magi.

HEROD

"Peace be to you. Welcome Princes, to our Kingdom."

SOTER

"Peace be to you. Greetings, O Great King Herod, from our Emperor and from us."

HEROD

"Thank you. I have seen the letter of your Emperor. I hope all is well with your Emperor and with you on your journey so far."

SOTER

"Yes, your Majesty. And we hope all is well with you, Your Majesty."

HEROD

"Yes, all is well. The letter speaks of a new born King of the Jews. You came to my palace seeking this new-born prince. How did you know of this wonderful event?"

SOTER

"Our council of astronomers and scientists spotted his Star when it arose in the East. The council designated us to travel on their behalf to greet this new-born king and report back to them. There is a prophecy in our scientific scrolls about this King of the Jews. They are desirous to confirm its fulfillment, O Great King."

HEROD

"How long ago did this Star appear to your astronomers?"

SOTER

"Precisely 25 months ago, by our calendar. That is, less than 2 years by your Roman calendar."

HEROD

"I have verified with the High Priests of the Temple. According to their prophecies the King of the Jews should be born in Bethlehem, which happens to be the home of King David, the once-famous and powerful King of the Jews."

SOTER

"Thank you, your Majesty. May we travel within your territory to this place called Bethlehem?"

HEROD

"Yes, Princes. You have safe passage. Go safely to Bethlehem. It is a very small village, about five stadia from here. Search diligently for the child. After you find and worship him, bring me word again, so that I too can come and worship him. In fact, all the Jews may go and worship him in Bethlehem."

SOTER

"Thank you, your Majesty. We will do as you desire."

The visitors are seen departing the Palace.

EXT   FIELD OUTSIDE JOSEPH'S HOUSE IN BETHLEHEM

SOTER

"Joseph, we do not know what intentions Herod had when he commanded us to return to him. He met with us by himself alone; there were no counselors, no advisers and no guards. He was acting quite nervous and secretive."

Pause.

SOTER

"Yesterday I received a vision from God. In my vision an angel warned me not to return to Herod. In obedience to **this** vision we are leaving Judea immediately by a different route. You too should take some precautions, Joseph. Peace be on you."

JOSEPH

"Thank you, sirs. Go in peace, and God go with you. Thank you for your blessings and for your kind gifts."

The Caravan commander comes toward them. SOTER makes a sign. As Joseph watches, the caravan quickly comes to life, and moves rapidly past Joseph out of sight into the night.

INT   JOSEPH'S HOUSE IN BETHLEHEM;

Joseph re-enters his house; Mary and the infant are asleep on the ground. Joseph sinks to the bedding on the ground and falls asleep.

Joseph hears his name being called.

AN ANGEL

"Joseph, Joseph."

Joseph wakes, is startled, turns his eyes toward Mary and the baby and turns toward the Angel.

ANGEL

"Joseph, Son of David. Herod is about to locate you, and kill your infant child. So pack up and leave immediately, tonight, and save yourself and the child. Do not go towards Judea, but go in the direction of Egypt and remain there till I bring you word again."

JOSEPH

"Sir, I am here for the Registration."

ANGEL

"Do not fear. The Registration will not take place. Obey God's command, and leave immediately."

DRAMATIZATION ENDS

INT   MATTHEW'S STUDY

Matthew is writing intently

JESUS

"When my parents returned from Egypt they stopped by in Bethlehem. My father made inquiries and learned that King Herod sent and killed all the male children in Bethlehem less than two years of age, according to what the Magi probably had told him. Thus, another prophecy was fulfilled."

Matthew looks up from his papyrus

JESUS

"So, Matthew, that is how I escaped the sword of Herod. Did you get all of it?

MATTHEW

"Yes, Master. This is a wonderful story; difficult to believe—unless you yourself narrated it to me."

JESUS

"Now do you understand why I directed you to keep these matters to yourself till I rise again from the dead?"

MATTHEW

"Yes, I do, Master. But then, how did you end up in Nazareth?"

JESUS

"An angel appeared to my dad Joseph in Egypt in a vision and told him that Herod was dead, and to get back to Israel."

Matthew starts writing again.

JESUS

"Herod was succeeded by his son Archelaus who was worse than Herod for cruelty. Therefore my dad was afraid to settle in Judea; he continued to Galilee and settled in Nazareth. There is a prophecy that the Messiah will be called a Nazarene. That was fulfilled."

Matthew hands a papyrus sheet to Jesus. Jesus begins reading it.

ACT 4

FOUNDATIONS OF
THE KINGDOM

INT   TAX OFFICE NEXT MORNING

Matthew reaches the tax office early, and is awaiting the arrival of Attalia (a senior official.)

MATTHEW
(Embracing Attalia)
"Peace be to you, Attalia, my friend."

ATTALIA
"Peace be to you, my friend. We enjoyed your feast yesterday. Is everything well with you?"

MATTHEW

"Yes, sir. I need your assistance for a personal matter. My friend the Rabbi whom I entertained yesterday is a descendant of David the King. Show me the genealogy scrolls of the Davidic family. His father is one Joseph from Bethlehem but settled in Nazareth."

ATTALIA

"Follow me."

He takes Matthew to a shelf of scrolls, looks down the rows and selects two.

ATTALIA

"There. These two scrolls have all about the family of King David. Come back to me if you have any questions."

Matthew takes the scrolls to his table. He sees Captain Arretus walking in, and goes to meet him.

ARRETUS
(Warmly)

"Matthew, welcome; we enjoyed your feast. Your Rabbi friend was the hero of the day."

MATTHEW

"Peace be on you, sir. I am happy to see you. I need a favor from you."

ARRETUS
(Humorously)

"Yes, Matthew, Ask me <u>anything</u>."

MATTHEW

"Sir, I want to take some time off to be with my Rabbi friend. He is fascinating."

ARRETUS
(Jokingly)

"What? Leave me? What will I do without you?"

They smile with each other. Arretus sits and makes himself comfortable on his couch.

ARRETUS

"Come, come. Now, Matthew, are you serious?"

MATTHEW

"Yes, Captain. I think this Rabbi will overturn our Jewish customs about ritual cleanliness and make our religion more reasonable."

ARRETUS

"What he spoke yesterday makes me think he will. But—he must be careful of these Pharisees. They are a nasty lot. Anyway, Matthew, you are a young man, and you can afford to take these risks. Go ahead and take time off. Get back when you finish with him. My good wishes go with you."

MATTHEW

"I am taking two of the genealogy scrolls. Attalia knows."

Arretus lifts his hand in approval.

INT   MID-DAY; MATTHEW'S STUDY

Matthew is reading the genealogy scrolls and making notes on a
papyrus. Jesus and five disciples arrive. Matthew goes out to greet
them and leads them to the dining room. The mid-day meal is
served. They all partake.

The meal is over.

JESUS
"Friends, Matthew is my disciple now. This will
diversify our group."

All the disciples smile and seem happy at this announcement.
From the dining room Jesus leads them to the front courtyard.

JESUS
"I plan to spend time updating Matthew about our
ministry. Till then you can get back to our place and
relax."

The disciples leave. Jesus and Matthew return to the study.

INT   MATTHEW'S STUDY

MATTHEW
"Master, I have summarized your genealogy. I brought
it down to fourteen names from Abraham to David,
fourteen from David to the exile and fourteen from
there to you. See this, please."

Matthew gives the papyrus to Jesus and leaves the study; he
returns shortly.

JESUS
(Handing back the papyrus)
"This is acceptable, Matthew."

Matthew takes the papyrus and binds it to a codex. He takes the codex, climbs into the attic and returns without it.

MATTHEW
"Rabbi, that codex will not be seen by anyone till you rise from the dead."

Jesus smiles.

MATTHEW
(Sitting down)
"Rabbi, yesterday you broke off after referring to a long discourse you made on a hillside in Galilee."

JESUS
"Yes, there was a very large crowd."

Matthew picks up a papyrus.

JESUS
"So I went up the hillside and my disciples came to me. Then I opened my mouth and taught them about the Kingdom of Heaven. 'Blessed are the poor in spirit, for theirs is the Kingdom of Heaven.'"

JESUS
"Blessed are they that mourn for they shall be comforted."

EXT   OUTSIDE SCENES APPEAR

The voice of Jesus is heard dictating the words. External scenes such as the animal yard are seen. Long shadows appear with the setting sun.

INT   MATTHEW'S STUDY

Matthew looks up from his papyrus.

MATTHEW
"Master, it is evening. Would you like to take a break now?"

JESUS
"Are you tired, Matthew?"

MATTHEW
"No, Master, we have worked several hours and a break will refresh us now. Let's go out for a few minutes."

They walk to the dining room and have some sweetmeats and drinks.

MATTHEW
"Jesus, master, I perceive that your philosophy is very much superior to that of the great Greek philosophers like Socrates or Plato or Aristotle."

JESUS
"Yes, Matthew, you have perceived correctly. Secular and pagan philosophy does not recognize that God is the source of human happiness. Humans cannot go to God by any amount of philosophy. God must come

down to mankind. He is doing that through me, my friend."

They walk back to Matthew's study.

Matthew lights a lamp, puts it on a lamp stand and takes up a papyrus and pen.

MATTHEW
"Yes, Master, please continue."

JESUS
"For if you do not forgive others their faults, neither will your heavenly Father forgive your faults."

EXT   **THE NARRATION MAY BE INTERSPERSED WITH EXTERNAL SCENES.**

JESUS
"Do not accumulate riches on earth where moth and rust destroys them and thieves break in and steal."

(Pause)

JESUS
"Then, Matthew I ended that long discourse with a parable: the one who hears and obeys my teachings is like a wise person who built a house on bedrock; it withstood the heaviest rain, winds and storms. The one who hears but does not obey them is like a foolish person who built a house on the sand. The rain descended and the floods came and the winds blew and beat upon that house and it fell—and great was the fall of it."

JESUS

"When I finished, the hearers were astonished at my doctrine, which was quite unlike the teaching of the Sadducees they had heard until then. Just like when you compared this doctrine to your Greek philosophers and teachers."

Matthew relaxes and applies ink to the papyrus. He then binds the codex and gives it to Jesus. Jesus appears to have read it, and hands it back to Matthew.

Matthew is seen taking the codex to his attic.

MATTHEW

"Master, we now have two codices up there."

JESUS

"I commend your diligence, Matthew. You are a faithful scribe."

ACT 5

THE KING SERVES HIS FLOCK

EXT   **GALILEE, A VILLAGE WELL**

Several ladies are gathered around the village well, filling earthen pots with water. There is gossip.

AYESHA

"Dedima has not returned. She left six days ago to see a new doctor in Petrea."

RACHAEL

"Won't she ever stop going to see new doctors? She's done this for years now."

KADEESHA

"Oh! She is a sad case. You know, her bleeding just won't stop. This is a mystery to everyone."

AYEESHA

"Ha, no mystery at all! I think she is demon-possessed. Demons work differently in men and women, you know?"

RACHAEL

"There, look up there. Is that Dedima returning from her trip?"

KADEESHA

"That's Dedima alright. I must find out what happened."

Kadeesha walks hurriedly towards Dedima. The other ladies follow and gather round the patient.

EXT   COURTYARD OF DEDIMA'S COTTAGE

AYEESHA

"So Dedima, we saw you arriving."

RACHAEL

"You seem to be quite cheerful. What did the new doctor tell you?"

AYEESHA

"Ah! You do not want to tell us?"

DEDIMA

"He charged me a lot of money and gave me some herbs to boil and drink, but did not guarantee a cure."

RACHAEL
"Why?"

DEDIMA
"He said this is a rare disease, for which there is no prescription, even in his medicine book."

Look of desperation on the faces of the ladies.

INT   CAPERNAUM; RESIDENCE OF JESUS AND HIS DISCIPLES

A centurion approaches them; some of his troops can be seen at a distance.

CENTURION
(Speaking to Jesus)
"Rabbi, Peace be upon you. My daughter is very sick, and, maybe, already dead, but please come and lay your hands on her and she will recover. I am convinced you can do this."

JESUS
"Yes. I will come with you. Take us there."

EXT   STREET LEADING TO CENTURION'S HOME

Jesus, his disciples and the centurion are walking forward, followed by soldiers. A crowd gathers by the roadside.

EXT   DEDIMA IS IN HER GARDEN

Deena comes rushing into the garden

DEENA

"Hey, Dedima, did you hear this? There is a miracle working Rabbi going to the centurion's house. A child is very sick or dead. Come on, we can watch."

Dedima follows with uneasy gait. Her face lights up as she catches sight of Jesus.

DEDIMA

"Deena, Is that the Rabbi? He looks so innocent and pure. I think this is the man who can actually cure me too. Shall I ask him?"

She goes towards the center of the street. Jesus is coming that way. He is now close by.

DEDIMA

"O, God! If I can even just touch his garment, I may be healed."

Jesus is going past her. She touches His garment. Immediately she stands erect, and smiles to Deena joyfully. Jesus stops.

JESUS
(Speaking to his disciples)

"Who touched me?"

PETER

"Rabbi, everyone is touching you. People are pressing us on every side, Master."

Jesus turns round and sees Dedima standing behind him. She looks at him radiant, smiling, in a guilty but child-like and contrite manner."

JESUS
(Speaking to Dedima)
"Daughter, your faith has made you well. Go in peace."

Dedima bows and smiles; the disciples look with surprise at Jesus' interaction with her.

BARTHOLOMEW
(Approaches Dedima)
"Lady, what did you do?"

DEDIMA
"Sir, I was sick for twelve years. No doctor could stop my bleeding sickness. Here, I merely touched his garment, and my bleeding condition has stopped immediately. I can now stand straight up like everyone else. He is a miracle worker, believe me.

Matthew is with Bartholomew and is seen writing on a tablet.

EXT   THE STREET; CONTINUED

Centurion's home comes into view. Plaintive music is heard.

INT   WITHIN THE CENTURION'S HOME

MOURNING LADY
(Sings a dirge; and others repeat each line in turns)
"Come all ye humans,
Mourn this little one,
So beautiful in death
As she was in life,
Separated a short time
Till in heaven we meet."

EXT   THE STREET

Jesus and the centurion arrive at the gate. DOMINATIO and his gang of burly men are there.

DOMINATIO
(Speaking to the Centurion)
"We have hired the best mourning ladies and the mourning is going on very well, Sir."

JESUS
(To Dominatio and bystanders)
"The child is not dead, but sleeps."

A BYSTANDER
"Ho, Ho, Ho, who are you, professor?"

2ND BYSTANDER
"Hey, man, from where did they get <u>this</u> doctor?"

3RD BYSTANDER
"Have we seen this medicine man before?"

The centurion walks to the gate. His troops line up behind him.

CENTURION
(To a soldier)
"Get the crowd out of the house."

Soldiers move into the house. The mourning ladies walk out briskly.

INT   CENTURION'S HOME

Jesus and the Centurion enter the house with the mother and siblings of the dead child. The disciples follow them in.

JESUS
(Speaking to the dead child)
"Little maid, arise."

The child shakes its hands and attempts to rise; the Centurion and a soldier quickly remove the coverings from the child. A gasp and a shout of joy erupt inside the house. Two soldiers rush out of the house.

EXT   OUTSIDE THE HOUSE

1ST SOLDIER
"He just told the child to get up. Look inside—there— our commander's daughter is now alive and seated on a chair."

2ND SOLDIER
"This is indeed a terrific thing. How did he do it?"

Dominatio and his gang are seen slowly leaving the scene.

Jesus' disciples are seen leaving the house. Matthew is seen holding a writing tablet in his hand.

EXT   A GREEN FIELD IN GALILEE;

It is late afternoon. There is a large crowd with Jesus

THOMAS
(Speaking to some disciples)

"It's getting late. Why don't we dismiss the crowd so they can find food in the villages round about?

BARTHOLOMEW

"Yes, good idea. Let's suggest it to Jesus."

They approach Jesus.

THOMAS

"Rabbi, it's getting late. Why don't we dismiss the crowd so they can go round the villages and buy food for themselves?"

JESUS
(Speaking very kindly)

"They need not go. You give them to eat."

THOMAS

"My God! You mean, to feed such a large crowd?"

JESUS
(Smiling benignly)

"Yes."

"How many loaves do you have?"

THOMAS

"There are only five loaves of bread and two small fishes around here."

JESUS

"Bring them here to me."

Thomas leads a small vendor boy, holding a basket containing the loaves and fishes. The boy has several empty baskets tied around his back—contents sold out. The disciples crowd round Jesus and the boy.

THOMAS
(Addressing the vendor boy)
"Give these to us. I will pay you."

The boy gives the basket to Thomas, and Thomas to Jesus.

JESUS
(Looking upwards)
"Abba, I Thank you for this food which you have given us out of your bounty; let it be sufficient for all your children gathered here. I bless this food in your loving name. Amen."

Jesus breaks one of the loaves. He asks the boy for an empty basket and places the second half in it. He places a fish in the other basket.

Jesus asks for more empty baskets and does the same again and again.

JESUS
(To the disciples)
"Friends, tell the multitude to sit on the grass."

Other vendor boys watching this give their empty baskets to Thomas. Jesus places loaves and fishes in each. Now there are many baskets with loaves and fishes.

The people nearest to Jesus start sitting on the grass. Gradually the people further away sit down on the grass.

JESUS
"Now start distributing the food."

The disciples keep distributing one loaf and one fish to each person. Two disciples reach the edge of the crowd; all the people have eaten something.

Peter and Thomas return to Jesus.

JESUS
(To Peter and Thomas)
"Pick up all the balance food, whatever remains. Do not waste any food."

MATTHEW
(To Bartholomew)
"How many people do you think are in this crowd, Bartholomew?"

BARTHOLOMEW
(Looking around)
"I guess there are at least five thousand, beside the womenfolk."

There is a glimpse of Matthew beside Bartholomew, with a tablet in his hand, surveying the crowd.

INT   EVENING; CAPERNAUM;

Residence of Jesus and the disciples; Peter, James and John are in conversation with Jesus.

JESUS

"Now, about the two parables which I taught you this morning; **(Pause)**

Did you understand them well, my friends?"

PETER

"Yes, we did, Master."

JESUS

"That is good, Simon. I have been reminding you often; the three of you are special for my ministry. Keep these two parables always in mind when this ministry suddenly falls on the three of you."

JAMES

"Rabbi, when will that happen?"

JESUS

"My father in heaven will decide that. I am training you to stand firm in faith. So, discuss today's two parables among yourselves and remember them always. You may leave now, Peace be upon you. As you go, please tell Judas Iscariot to come over for a conversation with me."

From a reclining position on a rug on the ground Peter, James and John rise and leave.

JUDAS ISCARIOT

"Master, you sent for me? Here I am."

JESUS

"Yes, Judas, my friend, walk in. Sit down and relax. I wanted to know how your tasks are going forward. Were you successful?"

Judas sits on the rug on the ground, on which Jesus is seated.

JUDAS ISCARIOT

"Yes, Master; I received a large number of contributions this week. I have put everything in the bag. **(Pause)** But I have no idea who these donors are. Anyway, I have enough in the Treasury for all our present needs, for food, rental expenses and everything."

JESUS

"So, Judas you have no concerns? That is good. If so, you can leave; as you go please tell Matthew that I need to see him. Thank you and peace be upon you."

Judas Iscariot rises and leaves.

MATTHEW

"Master, Judas conveyed your wish. Here I am."

JESUS

"Yes, Matthew, walk in."

Matthew sits on the rug beside Jesus. Jesus gives Matthew a codex.

JESUS

"This is acceptable. Thank you, Matthew."

MATTHEW

"Yes, Master. With this I now have seven codices."

JESUS

"Matthew, I am about to leave Galilee and embark on my final journey to Jerusalem. So, go home, leave these codices and bring a supply of fresh papyri. You will need plenty in Jerusalem."

MATTHEW

"Yes, Master. I will leave tomorrow and return the next day. Peace be upon you."

JESUS

"Peace be upon you, Matthew. As you go, please tell Thomas and Bartholomew to see me. Thank you."

Matthew rises and leaves.

Thomas arrives in Jesus' room.

THOMAS

"Master, Bartholomew and I are here. Matthew gave us the message."

JESUS

"Yes, walk in, my friends, thank you. Sit down and relax."

Thomas and Bartholomew sit on the rug beside Jesus and recline.

JESUS

"I need to share my plans with you. We are preparing to leave Galilee and go on to Jerusalem for the feast.

We will need places to stay and do ministry on the way, and at Jerusalem. Would you arrange these, please?"

THOMAS

"Yes, Master. What towns or villages do you wish to stay and do ministry?"

JESUS

"Find a village or town beyond the Jordan and a place to stay, for ministry. From there we will return to Jericho. Select a comfortable residence in Jericho. Next select a place between Jericho and Bethany. Say ten days at each place. At Bethany we have Simon the Leper; in Jerusalem we have a choice of places. Discuss all these with Simon. He will direct you. Then, discuss estimated expenses with Judas Iscariot. Thank you, my friends. My peace and blessings are with you in all these tasks."

ACT 6

THE KINGSHIP
IN DISPUTE

EXT   **STREET IN JERUSALEM**

Jesus is riding a young colt, surrounded by a crowd waving palm
branches

                       CROWD (shouting)

"Messiah"

"Son of David"

"Messiah"

Some residents of Jerusalem come out of their homes, on to the
street.

JERUSALEMITES
(Shouting to the procession)
"Who is this?"

FROM THE CROWD
(Shouting back)
"This is Jesus the Prophet of Nazareth of Galilee."

OTHERS IN THE CROWD
"This is Jesus the prophet of Nazareth of Galilee."

There is a brief view of Matthew writing on a tablet. The procession approaches the Temple. Jesus descends from the colt.

INT   NEXT DAY; WITHIN THE TEMPLE; HIGH PRIEST'S CHAMBER

Several Pharisees, Sadducees, students and their professors are gathered.

HIGH PRIEST
"Welcome, elders of the people and scholars. This is not a good time for our beloved Temple. You have witnessed what happened in the Temple yesterday."

Silence

HIGH PRIEST
"Now, tell me, who gave this so-called prophet of Nazareth the authority to overturn long established customs and disturb the merchants in the Temple?"

(Pausing and Looking around)

Tell me, from where will the people buy purified animals for sacrifice if there are no merchants to sell them?"

Silence

HIGH PRIEST

"They tell me that this so-called prophet has healed some lame and blind persons, who are now making a hero of him. Why are these lame and blind people in the temple anyway?"

A PHARISEE

"Actually the Temple is being polluted by sick people. I think we should prohibit lame, sick, blind and disabled people from entering the temple, at least during the festival."

HIGH PRIEST

"That is a very good suggestion. Go ahead and implement it; command the guards."

Two Pharisees leave the chamber.

HIGH PRIEEST

"Now turning to the main problem, what are we to do with this so-called prophet? He is disturbing the peace. If <u>we</u> punish him, these foolish common people may blame us. So, we need the Roman authority to step in and take care of him, don't you think?"

ABIRAM (a student)

"Sir, the Governor is in town. Why not accuse this prophet of causing sedition against the Emperor, and let the Governor deal with him; then our people will not blame us and we will be rid of him."

HIGH PRIEST

"That is a practical suggestion. How can we get that done?"

EL-JOSH (A Pharisee)

"Sir, let me suggest a plan. We can attend this man's teaching session and ask him whether it is lawful for us Jews to pay tribute to Caesar. If he answers "yes", we can accuse him to the people as a traitor, and if he says "no" we can accuse him to the Governor. What do you think, Sir?"

HIGH PRIEST

"That is a realistic idea.

(Pause)

Alright; you Pharisees, Professors and scholars arrange it among yourselves. Get me the evidence with credible witnesses. Go ahead. Peace be upon you and success attend you."

INT   A LARGE CHAMBER IN THE TEMPLE

Jesus is teaching; worshippers are listening; some Professors, students and Pharisees file into the chamber.

JESUS

"As I was saying, in my Father's Kingdom all people are equal. It is a very happy and blessed kingdom."

EBENEZER

(A Pharisee, stands up and looks round earnestly at the attendees and towards Jesus)

JESUS

"Yes, Rabbi, what is on your mind?"

EBENEZER

"Teacher, I notice that you speak very well because you do not care about individuals but speak your message boldly. Tell us your opinion; is it lawful to pay tax to the Emperor?"

Pause. There is rustling and gentle sound of admiration among the audience, as if Jesus is stumped.

JESUS

"Why are you testing me in this manner, like a hypocrite? Someone show me the money used to pay the Roman tax."

A member of the audience pulls out a money-bag, and a coin from it. The coin is passed from hand to hand to Jesus.

Jesus looks intently at the coin.

JESUS

"Whose is this image and this inscription?"

EBENEZER
"Of course, that is the emperor's."

Pause

JESUS
"So,

Pause

Give the emperor what belongs to the emperor, and
give to God what belongs to God."

**There is a gasp among the audience. Animated gesticulation
follows.**

**The disciples look at the group of Pharisees. The casual
worshippers smile at the Pharisees and at their students. Matthew
is seen on a side of the chamber writing on a tablet.**

INT   A SMALLER CHAMBER IN THE TEMPLE;

**Jesus is concluding a dispute with some Sadducees. More
Pharisees and students file into the chamber.**

JESUS
"In the resurrection they neither marry, nor are given
in marriage, but they are similar to the angels of God
in Heaven. Therefore, you are mistaken about the
resurrection."

**Sadducees are shown shaking their heads dissatisfied with the
conclusion. The Pharisees smile in approval. Some Sadducees are
seen leaving the chamber.**

Jesus turns to the group of Pharisees who remain.

JESUS

"Now, tell me about the Messiah. Whose Son is He?"

(Sound of murmuring among the Pharisees.)

ELIHU (A Pharisee)

"The Messiah is the Son of David."

JESUS

"Are you sure?"

JONATHAN (A Pharisee)

"Yes, teacher; it is so written, the Messiah is the Son of David."

All the Pharisees shake their heads in unison showing their agreement and approval.

JESUS

"How could you say that?

(Pause)

In the Psalms David himself by inspiration, says 'The Lord said unto My Lord, sit on my right hand till I make your enemies your footstool.'

Now, if David calls him Lord, how can he be his son?"

The Pharisees look at each other in surprise. Rustling noise is heard. Attention of casual worshippers and disciples is drawn to the group of Pharisees. Matthew is seen writing a tablet. Some Pharisees slowly leave the chamber.

ACT 7

A GOVERNOR ON TRIAL

INT   AN UPPER ROOM; TABLE IS LAID.

Jesus and the disciples are seated for dinner. Bartholomew and Thomas bring two goblets of wine, leave them on the table and take their seats.

JESUS
"Abba, we thank you for this beautiful food which you have provided for us out of your bounty. We bless this food in your loving Name."

Jesus takes a loaf of unleavened bread; he looks round the table and tears it in two.

JESUS
"My friends, this is my body which is broken for you. Do this whenever you eat it in remembrance of me."

Jesus gives half to each seated on either side. The other disciples take bread, break and share with each other.

Dinner is over. Jesus takes the bowl of wine in both hands. Disciples become silent.

JESUS

"Abba, we bless you for this pleasant wine which you have given us out of your bounty. We bless it in your loving name."

JESUS
(Looking round the table)

"My dear friends, drink this, all of you, for this is my blood of the <u>new</u> covenant which is shed for you and for many, for the forgiveness of sins. Do this whenever you drink it in remembrance of me."

He sips the vessel and passes it to John who sips and passes it to Thomas and so round the table.

The disciples are seen descending from the upper room and follow Jesus outside.

EXT   THE GARDEN OF GETHSEMANE;

Jesus is praying; drops of perspiration are flowing down his face; Peter, James and John are sleeping twenty feet away; other disciples are lying on the ground further away. Jesus rises and walks towards Peter.

JESUS

"Now take your rest. Don't you see the betrayer has arrived?"

Temple soldiers and a mixed crowd appear. They carry lanterns, spears and clubs. The disciples who were sleeping further away now run towards Jesus.

A man, his face covered in a shawl, steps from the crowd; he rushes towards Jesus and embraces him.

JUDAS ISCARIOT
(Embraces Jesus)
"Master, Master,"

JESUS
"Judas, are you betraying the Son of Man with a kiss?"

Two soldiers move rapidly to Jesus' side and hold him by his upper arms. Other soldiers move to isolate Jesus from the disciples.

A SOLDIER
(To the captain)
"Captain, who else should we arrest? What about this man's disciples?"

The disciples disappear into the darkness.

EXT   A DARK ALLEY IN JERUSALEM

Some disciples gather here

BARTHOLOMEW
"How did Judas collect these soldiers so soon after supper?"

THOMAS

"He must have arranged it beforehand. The story will come out tomorrow."

BARTHOLOMEW

"What a <u>bad</u> man; to betray Jesus like that!"

A Galilean rushes by, recognizes them, stops and gasps out:

GALILEAN # 1

"John and Peter are in the Chief Priest's palace. The Chief Priests are looking for witnesses to prove blasphemy against Jesus."

A second Galilean rushes by and stops

GALILEAN # 2

"They have condemned Jesus to death for Blasphemy. A Temple Guard told me. This is the end of Jesus."

A third Galilean rushes past and stops:

GALILEAN # 3

"Have you heard? Jesus is condemned to death."

MATTHEW

"Look. <u>They</u> cannot put Jesus to death. They must get a decree from a Criminal Court to do that."

GALILEAN # 3

"Sure. The Governor is in town. They are collecting a crowd to go there in the morning, and demand the death penalty."

The disciples join up with a crowd of Galileans. All are seen talking to each other; there is confusion.

Matthew draws Bartholomew aside by his arm:

BARTHOLOMEW

"You see what is happening, Matthew?"

MATTHEW

"Yes. See, they are collecting a crowd to go to the Governor in the morning. They need an order from him to kill Jesus. Why can't we warn the Governor?"

BARTHOLOMEW

"Are you mad, Matthew? How can we even get near the Governor? Besides, will he listen to you? Who are you? Are you the High Priest? Can you tell anything to the Governor?"

MATTHEW

"Why, Bartholomew, I am a Tax collector, on leave from the tax office at Capernaum. Therefore, I am a servant of the Governor and of Caesar. I can speak to him in Latin, his language. If I can get into the palace I can warn one of his counselors, or advisors or bodyguards, and they will warn the Governor."

BARTHOLOMEW

"Nonsense! That is the most scatter-brained suggestion I ever heard in my life. Drop it. Let's find out what is happening. Lots of rumors are flying around. Let's listen."

MATTHEW

"No, Bartholomew. You are my friend. I never asked any of you people for a favor. Do me this favor only. Just accompany me. I will try to get into the Governor's gate. If I succeed, I can warn someone. You can get back. At least we must do something for Jesus. Do not fear. Please come with me."

INT DISCIPLES' RESIDENCE, UPPER ROOM

Matthew and Bartholomew come in hastily. Matthew changes clothes; he puts on a tunic to look more like a Roman.

EXT STREET IN JERUSALEM

Matthew and Bartholomew descend to the ground and walk on. It is dark. The Governor's gate comes into view. They see soldiers round the palace.

MATTHEW

"Bartholomew, my friend, stop here. Let me now go alone. Watch me. If you see me going in, you return to our friends."

EXT RESIDENCE OF THE ROMAN GOVERNOR

Matthew is walking hurriedly alone towards the gate; he addresses the guards:

MATTHEW

"Hail!"

SOLDIER
(Points his spear at Matthew)
"Stop. This is the Governor's residence! Who are you?"

Matthew stands still.

MATTHEW
"I am a tax official from Capernaum. I need to give some secret information to the Governor's Counselors."

SOLDIER
"Not at this time. They are asleep."

MATTHEW
"This is urgent. Send a message to a Counselor."

SOLDIER
"Aren't you a Jew? How then do you speak Latin?"

MATTHEW
"I said I am a tax official. I was educated in Athens. I know the Law. This matter is serious for the Counselors."

SOLDIER
"What kind of secret?"

MATTHEW
"A tumult is brewing in Jerusalem tonight."

The Guards converse with each other. One guard is seen hastening into the Governor's residence. He returns; makes a motion to the other guards; then motions to Matthew to follow him. The soldier enters the gate, Matthew follows.

SOLDIER

"There, go round that corner. The Centurion will hear you."

INT   **THE GOVERNOR'S RESIDENCE**

Matthew walks round the corner and sees the Centurion.

MATTHEW
(Addressing the Centurion)

"Hail! My name is Matthew. I am a tax collector on leave from Capernaum. I want to inform the Chief Counselor about a possible tumult by the Jews today."

CENTURION

"What do they want?"

MATTHEW

"The Jews want a man executed by the Governor without evidence. They are collecting a big crowd for a tumult if he refuses."

CENTURION

"How do you know?"

MATTHEW

"I am a student of this Rabbi who favors paying tax to the Emperor. I have the evidence written, here."

(Matthew points to a codex in his pouch.)

CENTURION

"You think this is urgent? I cannot disturb the Chief Counselor. I will get an assistant. Stand here. Do not move."

The centurion returns with DECIUS, the assistant counselor.

MATTHEW

"Hail! My name is Matthew. I am a tax collector on leave from Capernaum. The Jews want to put a man to death without any evidence because he spoke in favor of paying taxes to Caesar, which the Jews treat as a crime. They are preparing a mob to cause a tumult. I came merely to warn you to be prepared for a tumult in the morning."

DECIUS

"Did you say your name is Matthew? Aren't you a Jew? How do you speak Latin well?"

MATTHEW

"I am a tax collector, servant of the Emperor. I was educated in Athens. I studied Law too there."

Decius gestures to Matthew to follow him, and shows a bench to sit on. Then he signals to a guard, points to Matthew (as if to keep an eye).

DECIUS

"The Governor is in bed. I will try to tell my Chief, AQUILA what you have told me. Stay right here. Do not move."

Matthew hears the sound of a crowd at the gate.

The Governor is up.

Matthew sees two Chief Priests and a Jewish official come into the building. The Governor is speaking to them. They leave.

INT   AN AUDIENCE ROOM IN THE PALACE

Pilate enters this audience room after dismissing the Jewish officials. He notices DECIUS walking by. DECIUS too sees Pilate and moves toward him.

PILALTE

"Decius, what got you up so early? Did you hear what these Priests are cooking up now?"

DECIUS

"Yes, Governor, I heard about it just now."

PILATE

"What is the urgency for a trial today, at this time? They can have it after their festival. Fetch me the Commander?"

DECIUS

"There, Governor, I see Commander Brassus just coming up."

PILATE

"How many men do you have, Brassus?"

BRASSUS

"Two hundred men, Honorable Governor."

PILATE

"Get all of them up here. Did you see a crowd at the Gate?"

BRASSUS

"Yes, Governor, that's why I was coming up when you looked for me."

PILATE

"The Priests want an urgent criminal trial. It's some sort of religious dispute. Can you control this crowd?"

BRASSUS

"Yes, I think so."

Pilate goes to a smaller conference room and is in conversation with Decius. AQUILA (Chief counselor) joins them a few moments later. Day is dawning. They hear the crowd returning.

PILATE

"Here they come. I think two High Priests are already in the ante-room. Brassus, hold them up till we are ready."

PILATE

"AQUILA, I may need your counsel at the Judgment Seat. This looks serious. I may need your opinion too, Decius."

Priests, Pharisees, Sadducees and Elders enter the building bringing Jesus bound. They enter the outer Hallway of the Hall of Judgment.

Pilate and the two counselors enter the Hall of Judgment.

DECIUS
(To Pilate and Aquila)

"Why do they need such a big crowd for a criminal trial?"

PILATE

"Decius, get me Brassus, quick."

Decius returns with the Commander.

PILATE

"Brassus, block the entrance. Allow only the leaders to enter this Hall of Judgment."

BRASSUS

"Yes, Governor. Now the crowd is much bigger."

PILATE

"These Jews always start a tumult when I am in town. They are determined to create a bad impression about my administration."

DECIUS

"Not you only, sir. They did that to your predecessors and I guess they will do it to your successors too."

Pilate ascends the Judgment seat. Aquila takes a lower seat at the right and Decius on the left. Soldiers bring the Chief Priests and Jesus into the Hall of Judgment.

A SOLDIER
"SILENCE IN THE HALL OF JUDGMENT!"

Pilate motions to put Jesus on the opposite side of the Hall. A Roman soldier leads Jesus to the right of Pilate.

PILATE
(Addressing the Priests)
"State your accusation."

HIGH PRIEST
"Honorable Governor, this man is a criminal. He is worthy of death."

PILATE
"Is that all? What is the crime he has committed?"

HIGH PRIEST
"He teaches blasphemous doctrines to our people, inciting them to rebel against the Temple, and against law and order; he has threatened to break down the temple and change our customs."

PILATE
"This is a religious dispute about your doctrines. I will not be a judge of religious matters. Take him away and judge him yourself."

2nd HIGH PRIEST
"Honorable Governor, according to our customs he should be put to death because he calls himself the King of the Jews."

PILATE
"Is that a crime?

(Pause)

"I will examine him."

PILATE
(Addressing Jesus)

"Are you the king of the Jews?"

JESUS
(Calmly)

"Are you saying so?"

PILATE

"See, how many things they are accusing you of? What is your defense to these accusations?

Jesus looks calmly at Pilate and a kind smile appears on his face.

PILATE
(Addressing the Priests)

"I need to confer with my counselors. Commander, move everyone to the ante-room; keep then under guard."

Six soldiers conduct the crowd to the ante-room (adjoining the Hall of Judgment).

Pilate descends the Judgment seat and goes to a small lounge behind.

INT   A SMALL LOUNGE

PILATE

"Aquila, I do not see any crime here. What do you think?"

AQUILA

"Neither do I. As usual, these Temple officials do not know the difference between civil and criminal law."

PILATE

"Tell you what, Aquila; during this festival I usually pardon a criminal. What if I tell them I want to set this man free? What is your opinion?"

AQUILA

"Sounds good to me; what do you think, Decius?"

DECIUS

"Yes. We cannot issue a death warrant without evidence of a crime, don't you think?

Pilate rises and returns to the Hall of Judgment. He ascends the Judgment seat. Aquila and Decius follow him below.

A domestic worker walks up from within the palace and whispers to Decius. From the judgment seat Pilate sees the domestic.

PILATE

"Yes, Dameter, what brings <u>you</u> in here?"

DAMETER
(Gets closer to Pilate on the Judgment seat)

"A message to you from your Lady, Honorable Governor."

PILATE

"A What? So unusual! What message would she send me at this time of day?"

DAMETER

"She tells you 'have nothing to do with that righteous man. I have been disturbed by many dreams tonight regarding him. Fare you well'."

PILATE
(Musing)

"Mighty Jupiter! How did <u>she</u> know I was dealing with anyone, let alone a righteous man? Decius, have you ever met a righteous man?"

DECIUS
(Smiling cynically)

"There is no such thing as a righteous man, Honorable Governor. All men act under the force of circumstances."

Pause.

PILATE

"Call in the parties."

Soldiers lead the crowd and Jesus into the Judgment Hall as before.

PILATE
(To the soldiers)

"There are a lot more people than previously. Who allowed them in?"

HIGH PRIEST

"Honorable Governor, all our elders are witnesses against this man. So we asked the Commander to let them in as witnesses. By your permission, Most Honorable Governor, all the residents of Jerusalem are perturbed why there is such a long delay in condemning this criminal. Therefore, many more have moved up here and are standing outside the Hall of Judgment and outside the building too."

PILATE

"I have consulted with my counselors. We Romans strictly divide criminal law from religious and civil law. This prisoner has done no crime worthy of death. So, I will make you an offer. At this festival it is my custom to release one condemned prisoner. I will release this man whom you have labeled as King of the Jews."

HIGH PRIEST

"No, Honorable Governor."

2ND HIGH PRIEST

"If you do release anyone, release Barabbas."

ELDERS, PHARISEES & SADDUCEES

"Yes, release Barabbas, not this man."

PILATE
(Startled)

"Then, what should I do with this prisoner whom you call King or Christ?"

HIGH PRIEST

"Let him be crucified."

PILATE

"What? (Silence) Crucify your King."

ELDERS, PHARISEES & SADDUCEES

"Yes, crucify him. Crucify him. Crucify him."

The crowd outside repeats (noisily and in a riotous manner)

CROWD

"Crucify him, crucify him, crucify him . . . ."

Pilate looks toward Aquila. Aquila rises and whispers to Pilate. Pilate turns his eyes towards the windows and sees the crowd; fear fills his eyes.

PILATE

"Decius, get me a bowl of water."

Decius walks past Matthew and returns with a tray, holding a silver bowl half full of water and a towel.

Pilate looks at the High Priest.

PILATE

"All of you want to crucify this man. I have examined him and find no fault in him. Here, I am washing my hands. His blood is not on my hands. I am not to blame for this judgment. You take that."

HIGH PRIEST

"His blood be on us, if that's what you mean, and on our generations."

PRIESTS AND ELDERS

"Yes, his blood be on us and on our children."

Decius removes the tray.

Pilate takes a pen and writes.

PILATE
"Decius, Fetch me Commander Brassus."

Decius walks to the street outside and returns with Brassus.

PILATE
"Commander, I have released the prisoner Barabbas by decree. The Temple authorities want him freed. They are responsible for it. Here is the writing."

(Pause)

"This man"

(Pointing to Jesus)

"The Temple authorities have demanded his crucifixion. I am innocent of this judgment. Here is the decree.

"And put this accusation on his head—'Jesus of Nazareth King of the Jews.'

Get it written in Hebrew and Greek too, and put it over his head."

2nd HIGH PRIEST
"Honorable Governor, do not write 'king of the Jews'. Write "he said he is the King of the Jews."

PILATE
"What I have written, I have written."

Pilate descends from the Judgment Seat and goes to the well of the court; he takes out a whip.

The Roman soldier takes Jesus and ties him to a pole on the left side of the Court.

Pilate strikes Jesus with the whip once. He stops.

Pilate returns and sits on the Judgment seat again.

PILATE
"Soldier, dismiss the court."

SOLDIER
"COURT IS DISMISSED!"

High Priests and Elders move out of the Judgment Hall, out of the building and to the street outside.

Roman soldiers take Jesus out of the Hall of Judgment towards their mess-hall within the Palace.

Pilate beckons to the Commander; then descends from the judgment seat and goes to the lounge behind.

PILATE
"Brassus, this man does not look like a criminal. Did you notice—he did not flinch at the whip? Perhaps he is a King of some sort."

(Pause)

"Get someone to carry his cross. Save him that indignity. Get the crowd out of the street, fast."

(Pause)

"And get the prisoner too out of this building."

Decius walks up to where Matthew remains seated.

DECIUS
"You said you are a tax official from Capernaum. You did not disturb the court, Thank you. There was no time to warn Aquila about this tumult, or the Governor. Anyway, thanks for trying."

They see Jesus coming from the soldiers' mess hall dragging a cross, and going across the Hall of Judgment.

MATTHEW
"Thank you, counselor for letting me into the Hall of Judgment. He was my beloved teacher. Let me go with this crowd. Thank you and farewell."

DECIUS
"Farewell."

ACT 8

THE KING COMPLETES
HIS MISSION

A troop of soldiers accompany Jesus, dragging the cross, on to the street outside. At the gate there is a donkey-cart stopped, waiting for the crowd to pass.

Two soldiers hasten toward the cart followed by a Centurion.

1ˢᵗ SOLDIER
"Hey, carter! What's your name?"

SIMON OF CYRENE
"Sir, I am Simon of Cyrene father of Alexander and Rufus. Why?"

SOLDIER
"Are you a Jew?"

SIMON OF CYRENE
"Yes, sir."

SOLDIER
"You are a strong young man. Go, take that cross from that prisoner, and carry it to the place of execution."

SIMON OF CYRENE
"What about my cart?"

SOLDIER
"Do as I say, fast."

Other soldiers gather round, and compel Simon to get off his cart and walk up to Jesus and carry the cross.

The execution procession moves a short distance, and is joined by another procession with two prisoners carrying a cross each. A group of Galileans joins the crowd. Jesus, now free of the cross is seen talking to folk in the crowd.

The soldiers are in formation. They move to the place of execution.

EXT   DAYBREAK GOLGOTHA

(PLACE OF EXECUTION)

The procession arrives. Two soldiers remove Jesus' cloak.

A SOLDIER
"This is a single piece of clothing, woven from top to bottom. Nice."

Several soldiers gather round and admire the cloak.

Three papyrus sheets are driven into the top of the cross meant for Jesus. Jesus is nailed to the cross; it is straightened into a hollow; servants fill the hollow with soil. Two others are crucified similarly and their crosses are raised on either side of Jesus.

HIGH PRIEST

"He said he is the Son of God. Let Him deliver him <u>now</u>, if he will have him!"

SECOND HIGH PRIEST

"If he is the King of Israel, let him <u>now</u> come down from the cross and we will believe him."

Some travelers are passing by. They stop at the site.

1st TRAVELER

"Oh, here is that magic-man. My God, he is crucified! So soon! He said he can break down the temple and build it in three days. Now, see what's happened to him!"

Matthew is seen near them, tablet in hand. The travelers move on.

Jesus makes a loud noise and suddenly his head hangs limp, on his neck. Galileans gasp in agony.

The roar of an earthquake is heard and the crosses shake. Suddenly the sky becomes dark.

1st SOLDIER
(Placing his hands on his head)

"Jupiter, save us!"

CENTURION
"Perhaps He was the Son of a God; who knows?"

JOSEPH OF ARIMATHEA arrives with a group of people. He beats his breasts with both hands.

JOSEPH OF ARIMATHEA
"How did this happen? Who gave the decree to crucify Jesus?"

A PRIEST (standing by)
"The Governor did. It was all done lawfully."

Joseph of Arimathea leaves.

EXT   GATE OF PILATE'S RESIDENCE;

Joseph of Arimathea arrives and speaks to the soldiers.

JOSEPH OF ARIMATHEA
"Hail. I am Joseph of Arimathea. I need to speak to the Governor. He knows me. This is urgent. Please inform him that Joseph of Arimathea is at the Gate."

A soldier leaves and then returns. He signals to the other guards to let him in.

Joseph enters Pilate's residence and walks confidently up to the lounge.

INT   **LOBBY OF PILATE'S RESIDENCE; AQUILA AND DECIUS ARE SEATED AND IN CONVERSATION WITH PILATE.**

JOSEPH OF ARIMATHEA

"Hail. Honorable Governor and Counselors, I am Joseph of Arimathea."

AQUILA

"Hail. Welcome. What brings you at this time?"

JOSEPH OF ARIMATHEA

"Honorable Governor, and counselors, you probably did not know that I am a disciple of this man, who has been suddenly crucified today. I believed that He is the Messiah, the Son O God, and SPIRITUAL KING of the Jews, and I hoped that he would change the customs of the Jews, and make us more like the rest of the world."

AQUILA

"It is too late for you to save your friend, or teacher or whatever. The whole city of Jerusalem was in tumult this morning, asking to crucify him."

PILATE

"Yes, Joseph. There was no criminal charge against him. They wanted him crucified because he said he is the King of the Jews. What's the problem with that? And they compelled me to order his crucifixion by threatening a tumult."

Pause

PILATE

"I was surprised, very surprised, when they asked me to free Barabbas instead. They gave me no choice."

JOSEPH OF ARIMATHEA

"He is dead. I came to beg his body for burial."

PILATE

"What? Already dead? That's impossible. Decius, summon a soldier."

Decius leaves the Lobby and returns with a soldier.

PILATE

"Soldier, go tell the commander that I want him to verify whether this prisoner, so called King of the Jews, is dead. Quick."

AQUILA

"If we did not crucify him, there would have been a full-scale tumult."

PILATE
(In frustration)

"I have done much for the Temple Jews, but nothing seems to satisfy them. There is some unrest whenever I come up here from Caesarea."

Pause.

Brassus appears with four soldiers.

BRASSUS

"Hail, Governor."

PILATE

"Hail."

BRASSUS

"Honorable Governor, I received your message. I have verified. That so-called King of the Jews is dead. This man"

(pointing to a soldier)

"speared him in the side. Blood and water came out. There is no doubt. My surprise is how quickly he died. Surprise, really."

PILATE
(To Joseph)

"You may have the body. Brassus let him take charge of the body of this so-called King of the Jews."

EXT   GOLGOTHA

Joseph of Arimathea and a soldier arrive. Joseph's servants are at the site. They dig out the cross, tilt it, take the body and place it on a flat bed and carry it away. They carry it a short distance, lay the body in a stone tomb, and slide a stone door across the opening.

INT   TWO DAYS LATER; THE UPPER ROOM: BEFORE DAWN

The disciples are asleep. Sound of excited female voices comes from the outside.

Some disciples get up and run down the steps to the pavement. Several ladies are talking animatedly; the disciples stand around them.

MARY MAGDALENE

"Early in the morning all of us went to the tomb to anoint His body. Actually we were worried how to push that big stone door. As we approached there was an earthquake and an angel came down from Heaven. We saw the angel with our own eyes. What a sight it was. He was shining and looked glorious. The door of the tomb just rolled aside and he sat on it. His face shone very brightly, more than the Sun, and he told us: 'Do not be afraid. You are seeking Jesus. He has risen from the dead as he told you. Go and tell his disciples that he goes before them into Galilee. They can meet him there.'

"We were really scared. And when we were running back to tell you, Jesus appeared and said 'All Hail.' Then we ran and worshipped him. He said "do not be afraid. Go and tell my brethren to go to Galilee. They can meet me there." So we ran back here to tell you all."

Peter and John start running towards the tomb. Matthew is seen running upstairs, grabbing his codex and writing on it hurriedly.

INT   THE UPPER ROOM; FEW DAYS LATER

Disciples are gathered together.

PETER

"Brethren, our Blessed Master has overcome death and risen from the tomb as he told us. The ladies saw him first. He gave them a commandment, that we proceed to Galilee where we will see him. We leave the day after tomorrow at dawn."

A murmur of approval and shaking of heads follows.

THOMAS
"Are all Galileans joining us?"

PETER
"No. Only we eleven will go. We will take only Barnabas and two others. We have no idea what Jesus will command us next."

EXT   **ROLLING HILLS OF GALILEE;**

The disciples are in a group of 14 males going up the hill.

MATTHEW
"Bartholomew, does Peter know where he is leading us?"

BARTHOLOMEW
"Yes. Peter received a vision to meet Jesus on this hillside. John told me that."

On his left Matthew hears three other disciples in conversation.

A DISCIPLE
"Do you think we will be meeting the same Jesus who was crucified or someone else?"

2nd DISCIPLE
"One can never be sure. What if it is a different person who looks like Jesus?"

3rd DISCIPLE

"We will know only when we actually meet him, don't you think?"

1ST DISCIPLE

"There, there, there he is. Looks like the same Jesus our beloved Master!"

They all run toward Jesus, fall down on the grass and worship him. Some disciples are wiping tears; others are trying to get his attention or to speak to him.

The disciples gather round him.

JESUS

"You are my friends and my beloved disciples. I have overcome death as I told you. You can now proclaim it. All authority is given to me in heaven and on earth."

Matthew is seen pulling out a tablet and a pen, and gestures as if he is about to start writing.

"Therefore, go and teach all nations baptizing them in the name of The Father, and of The Son and of The Holy Spirit."

JESUS

"Lo, I am with you always even unto the end of the age!"

Jesus goes round the group talking to each of them individually.

The disciples are seen descending the hillside.

ACT 9

THE SYNOPTIC PUZZLE BEGINS

INT   MATTHEW'S HOME IN CAPERNAUM

Matthew is seen washing his feet and entering his home; he is met by three children; he embraces them in turn, enters and greets his wife.

MATTHEW
"Nabeeda, they killed Jesus, my beloved Master."

Nabeeda gasps, then presses the palms of her hands to her face.

NABEEDA
"Oh God! Who killed him?"

MATTHEW

"The Jewish priests."

NABEEDA

"How did they kill him?"

Matthew sits on a chair, rests his head on his hands and tells her in a breaking voice:

MATTHEW

"They arrested him in the night and took him to the Roman Governor. They collected a large crowd that same night and threatened to create a tumult if Jesus is not crucified. The Governor became afraid and crucified Jesus."

NABEEDA

"When did this happen?"

MATTHEW

"Last Friday. On the Feast day!"

(Pause)

"But do you know what happened? Two days later Jesus miraculously walked out of the tomb alive. Those Galilean ladies were there and saw the tomb opened, and they met Jesus afterwards. Can you believe it? Nobody thought that it will actually happen like this, even though he told us many times and I had written it several times."

NABEEDA

"Did you meet him or speak to him afterwards?"

MATTHEW

"Yes. He told us to go to Galilee. We came from Jerusalem and met him today. He gave us commands. Then he spoke with each one us. He told me to keep the writings safely till he returns. The disciples went back to Jerusalem. I came home. I am not comfortable in their company without Jesus."

NABEEDA
(Gently)

"We had a message from Captain Arretus, asking about your health."

Matthew stands up.

MATTHEW

"Nabeeda, I am feeling somewhat unwell. Let me rest a bit."

Matthew goes to a bed and lies down.

EXT   AFTERNOON; CAPERNAUM

Three months later. Street outside Matthew's home. A group of visitors appear at the gate; a male domestic greets them.

DOMESTIC

"Welcome, Sirs. What can I do for you?"

BARTHOLOMEW

"We have come from Jerusalem searching for Matthew our friend. He used to live in this house."

DOMESTIC

"Welcome, sirs. He is at work at the Tax Office. But he will be home soon. Here is water; wash your feet. Let me take your donkeys to the yard."

BARTHOLOMEW

"Thank you."

INT   INSIDE MATTHEW'S HOME

The domestic places refreshments for them.

He re-appears at the door, with Matthew behind him.

DOMESTIC

"These are the visitors, master."

They all stand. Matthew recognizes one of them and rushes to embrace him.

MATTHEW

"Peace be upon you, Bartholomew, my true friend. I am so happy to see you again. Who are your friends here?"

BARTHOLOMEW

"Peace be upon you, Matthew, my friend. Greetings! Let me introduce them."

"This is MARCUS. He is a nephew of Simon and also of Barnabas. Do you remember Barnabas?

This is LUCAS, a medical doctor who is now a member of our Sect. This is Demetrius, originally from Cyprus and now a member of our Sect in Jerusalem."

Matthew embraces each of them warmly when introduced.

DOMESTIC
"Master, I am serving dinner."

MATTHEW
"Friends, I welcome all of you to my humble home and to dinner?"

They all move to the dining room and are seated around the table.

MATTHEW
"Bartholomew, shall I bless this food?"

BARTHOLOMEW
"Yes. Please do."

MATTHEW
"Abba, we thank you and bless this food in remembrance of your Son Jesus our Messiah, our Savior, just as he commanded us."

Matthew breaks one loaf of bread and gives half to Bartholomew. They all start eating.

BARTHOLOMEW
"Matthew, why did you not return to Jerusalem with us after our trip to Galilee?"

MATTHEW
"I was very, very depressed at the loss of Jesus. I knew I would be discriminated by you people; you always treated me as a tax collector."

BARTHOLOMEW
(Smiling)

"Matthew, my friend, that is a perception in your own mind only. None of us discriminated against you. At least you know I was your friend all the time. I am distressed to hear you say that."

MATTHEW

"The Captain of the Tax Office invited me back, and so I have re-joined my old job."

MATTHEW

"So, now, what brings you to Galilee? If you or your friends are having tax troubles I could fix them for you?"

BARTHOLOMEW

"Oh no, no! Matthew, I will have no tax troubles in future. I have sold everything and given it to our community in Jerusalem. None of us have any property anymore, so no tax troubles!"

MATTHEW

"Really? Sold everything? I could not have done that, you know. My property belongs to my family. It was probably a good thing I did not stick on with our sect."

MATTHEW

"Then, what brings you here?"

BARTHOLOMEW

"Lucas here will tell you better than I can."

LUKE

"Matthew, it is nice to meet you. Thank you for your kindness and hospitality. I was present at the Crucifixion of Jesus and was greatly impressed by what happened. I am now a baptized member of the sect of the Nazarenes. Our sect is growing very fast. We need literature to inform new believers about Jesus. Mark here has written a short narrative of whatever Peter remembers. I am writing a more comprehensive treatise about Jesus for the large number of converts."

MATTHEW

"How did you set about it?"

LUKE

"Mary, the mother of Jesus was in our company and she told us about the miraculous birth and childhood of Jesus. I wrote everything, everything. I even took a trip to Judea to interview Zacharias and Elizabeth to check out what Mary told us."

LUKE

"Afterwards, I wrote what I remembered of the crucifixion. The disciples told me what they remembered of events in Jerusalem; I cross-checked their narratives with reliable witnesses."

Luke sips wine.

"However, none of them could remember details of Jesus' teachings. They told me snatches of parables and miracles which Jesus did in Galilee. I could not write those bits and pieces."

LUKE

"I was perplexed. Then, last week Bartholomew mentioned that you were writing notes while in their company. He is the one who suggested this trip. Tell me, Matthew, what happened to any notes that you wrote at that time?"

MATTHEW

"Yes, Lucas."

Pauses; becomes emotional.

"They are safe and hidden away."

Matthew lowers his head and rests them on his palms. He seems to be sobbing silently. The others stare in surprise and wait for him to recover.

LUKE

"Matthew, you are my brother in Jesus, I respect your emotions. I think my treatise will be a great help in spreading knowledge about Jesus among new believers. Would you mind sharing your notes with me?"

MATTHEW

"Yes, Lucas. I must share my notes with you. Actually, Lucas, I feel very sad whenever I think about Jesus. In my job as a tax collector, I meet all sorts of people. Jesus was unlike anyone else. He had no desire for wealth. There was no envy, anger or fear and there was no falsehood in him. He was so lovable, and he loved everyone equally. When I was with him I forgot that I was a tax collector or a publican or an outcast of the Jews. He was not an ordinary human. From the first day

I sensed that he was the Son of God. Let's get to work on my notes after dinner."

Dinner ends. Matthew leads them to his study.

MATTHEW

"Lucas, you said that you need the teachings and miracles of Jesus in Galilee."

While they watch, Matthew takes a lamp, climbs the stairs and opens the trap door. He disappears into the attic and returns with some codices in his hand. He places them on a table.

MATTHEW

"Lucas, see whether these are what you want."

LUKE
(Opening one and looking)

"Yes, Matthew, these are exactly what I need. They are orderly and detailed; very good. May I make a copy?"

MATTHEW

"Yes. Let me set up that table for you."

Matthew sets up papyrus, pen, ink and cloths on a table; Luke starts copying.

MARK
(Reading a codex and fingering
a sheet of papyrus)

"Uncle Matthew, these papyri sheets are excellent quality. We don't get such good stuff in Jerusalem. From where did you get these papyri?"

MATTHEW

"Our tax office has a good supplier. These papyri were manufactured in Lower Egypt. See, both recto and verso are excellent. I used the best quality to write notes for Jesus. Of course they cost more."

MARK

"You have written some things that my Uncle Simon seems to have forgotten. Uncle, may I also copy some of your notes? I can add them to my codex, if my Uncle Simon does not object."

MATTHEW

"Yes son, please do."

Matthew sets up a table for Mark. Mark starts copying. Matthew sits down at Luke's table.

LUKE

"Matthew, you were a disciple of Jesus. Looks as if you wrote these on a daily basis, did you?"

MATTHEW

"Yes, Lucas. I wrote these similar to my diaries at the tax office. My model was Xenophon. I tried to imitate the simple style of the Anabasis. Of course I wrote only what Jesus signaled me to write. Many events and teachings were left out."

LUKE

"Did Jesus ever see these?"

MATTHEW

"Yes. Jesus met with each of us individually. When I finished a codex I gave it to him, maybe once every three or four weeks. He approved or made corrections before I put them away."

LUKE

"These are very detailed and sequential indeed, Matthew. Do you have any intention of publishing them?"

MATTHEW

"Lucas, I wrote these codices according to his wishes. He is the owner. I cannot do any such thing unless he directs me. At our last meeting he told me to keep them safely till his return."

LUKE

"You are a faithful scribe, Matthew. Your diaries may be useful to spread the good tidings that Jesus preached."

EXT   NEXT DAY

Street facing Matthew's home. Visitors bid farewell to Matthew and to his domestic.

MATTHEW

"Fare you well, my friends. Let the memory of Jesus be with us always."

They leave, with their donkeys following them.

ACT 10

THE DIARIES RETURN
TO THEIR MESSIAH

INT   SEVERAL DECADES LATER

Matthew is now an old man. He is resting on a bed.

Matthew's grandson ADAM arrives. He is a young man about twenty years of age. Adam sees Matthew and rushes to embrace him.

ADAM
"Grandpa, peace be upon you. I got your message three days ago. How's your health? Nothing too bad, I hope."

MATTHEW
"My son, sit down. Relax. Have a drink.

Pause

How is your business? I am relieved that you got into business so early in life. You are not a tax official like me or my son, your dad, or like my forefathers before me."

ADAM

"My business is doing well, grandpa. We sent a consignment of jars to the Roman market yesterday. That is what delayed my arrival."

MATTHEW

"I am happy to hear that. Son, thank you for visiting me now. Something has been worrying me for more than ten years. Is this a good time to discuss it with you?"

ADAM

"Yes, grandpa. I am here for you."

MATTHEW

"Adam, you are now a grown man and you can understand."

ADAM

"What is it grandpa?"

MATTHEW

"Son, can you keep a secret?"

ADAM
(Puzzled)

"Yes, grandpa. Why?"

MATTHEW

"My beloved boy, when I was your age, or a bit older, the Messiah appeared suddenly and called me. I became his disciple."

"I kept diaries for him, like my old tax records. I wrote whatever he wanted. The Priests in Jerusalem crucified him and then buried him, but he walked out of the grave alive three days later. Then he met with us; he told me to keep the diaries safely until he returns."

MATTHEW

"The time is coming, my son, when I will go to be with my fathers. When I am gone, Adam, I want you to keep those diaries safely for my Messiah."

ADAM

"Yes, Grandpa, I will. But, how am I to recognize him?"

MATTHEW

"Son, his appearance, his language and his demeanor will tell you instantly that it is he; and he knows you. He is the Son of God. You know what? He came to our office suddenly and called me by name. How did he know me or that I would gladly become his follower?"

ADAM

"Alright, grandpa. Where are the diaries you are talking about?"

MATTHEW

"Let me show you."

Matthew slowly rises and leads the way to his study. He walks to the stairs, places one foot on it and points to the trap door above.

MATTHEW

"They are all in there. Some time when you are free, just walk up and take a look. I have removed all the secret tax records. Only the Messiah's diaries remain there."

ADAM

"Alright, Grandpa. I will do as you say. But I have something to talk to you about. May I do so, now?"

Matthew sits. Adam sits beside him.

MATTHEW

"Yes, son. You can ask me anything. You are my beloved grandson. I am all yours."

ADAM

"In my city there is a colony of people who say they are followers of the Messiah. My friends hate them and want to put them to death. Is this the same Messiah that you are also talking about, Grandpa? They are also called Christians."

MATTHEW

"Adam, my son, we were the sect of the Nazarenes because the Messiah was from Nazareth in Galilee. Someone invented the name Christians which, after all, is Greek for Messiah. Yes, Adam, it must be the same Messiah, Jesus the Christ."

ADAM

"Thank you Grandpa."

MATTHEW

"Now that you asked me, Son, I have my own question about them. Do these Christians still consider tax collectors as ritually unclean? That's why I left them."

ADAM

"These Christians, they have no idea about ritual cleanliness like us. They eat anything like the gentiles. They treat everyone equally but they are very funny, grandpa, they can marry only one wife! But they are very good to each other. That is amazing!"

MATTHEW

"It should not be so amazing, Adam. That is what Jesus used to teach us. He wanted us to love each other like brothers and to forgive each others' mistakes. Actually, He did not teach us to eat everything. But he loved the gentiles and Jews equally."

ADAM

"Thank you grandpa; It was nice talking these things with you."

MATTHEW

"Son, I have gifted this house and all its lands to you. The deeds and conveyances have been properly registered in your name. After I am gone, look after Pereus. He has served me faithfully almost ten years. Let him live off these fields and gardens. And safeguard those diaries till my Messiah comes asking for them."

ADAM

"Yes, grandpa; I will treat Pereus honorably. Actually, I like him. He is obedient and polite."

MATTHEW

"Adam, I bless you, my son. You are a jewel to my family. Let my blessings be with you always."

ADAM

"Thank you grandpa; I hope you are feeling better, now, are you?"

MATTHEW

"Yes, my son, talking these matters with you has actually improved my health. I feel stronger and happier now."

INT   ANTIOCH; SEVERAL DECADES LATER

A gathering of Christians is ending.

PRESIDER

"And so, brethren, Go in peace. Let us all be joined together in brotherly love, in the name of our Lord and Savior Jesus Christ. Amen."

The conference breaks up. VARIANUS walks up to the Presider.

VARIANUS

"Greetings, Holy Father."

PRESIDER

"Greetings, my son; you seem eager to say something to me. Speak on."

VARIANUS

"Yes, Holy, Father, I was excited when you spoke about the search for old writings about Jesus."

PRESIDER

"What is the reason for your excitement?"

VARIANUS

"I am the delegate from Capernaum, Holy Father! Jesus started his ministry in my city. There are many stories about him there. A tax collector of Capernaum named Matthew was a disciple of Jesus."

PRESIDER

"That is already well known among us, my son."

VARIANUS

"My friend Antonio, a fellow-Christian is now the caretaker of Matthew's old house. He told me that the house is full of old scrolls. Maybe there is something about Jesus in some of those scrolls?"

PRESIDER

"Have you seen their contents?"

VARIANUS

"No, Holy Father. I cannot read. Antonio too cannot read."

PRESIDER
(Looking toward another priest)
"Father George!"

(Pause)

"Father George!"

FATHER GEORGE turns round.

PRESIDER

"This young man has some news for you, Father George. My son, please go with Father George and tell him everything. Thank you and go in peace."

Father George takes Varianus and moves out of the crowd.

EXT   CAPERNAUM; A WEEK LATER

Father George arrives at Varianus' house in Capernaum with four young scholars. Father George leaves the scholars there, and sets off with Varianus. Two donkeys follow them.

EXT   PELLA, A TOWN IN THE DECAPOLIS

Varianus and Father George reach the Fourth house on River Jordan Street in Pella. They knock and make a noise on the outer gate. A domestic worker comes out.

FATHER GEORGE

"Hail. My name is George. I am looking for one Adam, a well known businessman with relatives in Capernaum."

Adam comes out. He is now very old.

ADAM

"Yes, friends, I heard you mention my name. I am Adam. Who are you?"

FATHER GEORGE

"Hail, and greetings, my dear sir. I am Father George, a servant of Jesus Christ the Messiah. I am from Antioch. My young friend here is Varianus, a Christian of Capernaum."

ADAM

"Welcome."

Adam offers them water for their feet and leads them indoors. The domestic leads their donkeys away. They are seated.

ADAM

"Yes, sirs, if you have come on business, you will be disappointed. I retired from business last year. My son, Julian has taken over. I can direct you to his place of business. But first have some food."

The domestic places sweetmeats, fruits, milk and wine on tables. They refresh themselves.

ADAM

"You said you are from Antioch. I have traveled to that city many times on business. I used to lodge at a nice Inn on a street called Sacred Street."

FATHER GEORGE

"Ah, ha! I know that Inn very well. Did you learn how that street got its name?"

ADAM

"No. No one ever mentioned it."

FATHER GEORGE

"A town councilor lived on that street. His child fell sick, very sick and was about to die. The presbyter of the Christian ecclesia nearby visited them and saw the child. He knelt and prayed beside the child and the child was cured miraculously. The whole family became believers of the Messiah. That councilor moved the City Council to change its name to "Sacred Street."

ADAM

"I once wondered what was so sacred about that street. Good to know this story. And so, sirs, what sort of business brings you to me?"

FATHER GEORGE

"I am a scholar, a teacher and leader among the Christian community in Antioch. Our founder was the Messiah, Jesus of Nazareth who was crucified by the Jews, but rose from the grave on the third day."

"Have you heard about the Messiah, sir?"

ADAM

"Oh."

"Yes. My grandpa gave me that large house in Capernaum as a gift. Then he said it contains some diaries. He said I was to give them to the Messiah when he comes."

Silence ensues while Adam seems to contemplate something.

ADAM

"Now I too am an old man. That house is very old too, over a hundred years, in fact. It needs to be pulled down. Maybe now I should hand over everything to <u>my</u> grandson."

FATHER GEORGE

"We Christians are the devoted followers of your grandfather's Messiah. Many of us have suffered death and martyrdom in His name. Would you consider it wise or prudent to make a copy of your Grandpa's diaries? Then they will not be lost even if the house crumbles or is demolished in the near future."

ADAM

"I don't know. Let us go to Capernaum and decide this matter there. It is late now. Stay on. Let us leave tomorrow morning."

Father George
(Falling to his knees)

"Lord Jesus Christ, my blessed Messiah, I thank you that you have given us grace in the sight of your servant Adam. Amen."

Adam looks at Father George, puzzled.

EXT   MATTHEW'S HOUSE IN CAPERNAUM

Adam, Father George and Varianus arrive.

FATHER GEORGE
(Turning to Varianus)

"Brother Varianus. Maybe it would be prudent if you continue your journey; go home and bring my student scholars here."

VARIANUS

"Yes, Father George."

Varianus continues his journey.

Adam and Father George remove their sandals and enter the gate. Antonio (the caretaker) greets them, gives them water to wash their feet. They enter the house. Antonio places refreshments for them. After refreshments they go to Matthew's old study.

ADAM

"Father George, do you see all these scrolls lying around? These are my grandpa's old tax records. They are more than sixty or seventy years old. Maybe I should send them off to his old tax office."

Pause

ADAM
(Going to the stairs)

"The Messiah's diaries are in that attic up there. Father George, can you read?"

FATHER GEORGE

"Yes, sir. I was educated in Greek, Latin, Hebrew, Aramaic and Farsi. In whatever language the diaries are written, I can read and copy them accurately, praise to my Lord Jesus Christ."

Varianus arrives with the four scholars. They join Adam and Father George in Matthew's study.

FATHER GEORGE

"Sir, these are my students. Brothers, this is Adam, the grandson of Matthew the tax collector and disciple of our blessed Redeemer and Messiah the Lord Jesus Christ.

ADAM

"Welcome. You talk about my grandpa as if you knew him well."

SCHOLARS

"Hail, and greetings from us, too."

A SCHOLAR

"Yes, sir. We all know about Matthew the disciple of Jesus. He is mentioned in our Holy Scriptures."

ADAM

"I am pleased to hear that. We are about to look at the diaries which my grandpa left for his Messiah. They are in that attic. It is pretty dark up there. Antonio, get us a lamp."

Antonio brings a lamp.

ADAM

"Antonio, have you been in that attic before?"

ANTONIO

"Yes, master, I clean it twice a year. I was instructed by my grandfather, your servant Pereus."

ADAM

"Go up there and bring down all the books that are on the little table."

ANTONIO
(Cheerfully)

"Yes, master."

Antonio disappears into the attic. He brings down three codices, goes back brings four, goes back again and brings four more. He leaves them on a table. (Each codex is small and contains 5 or 6 papyri sheets.)

ADAM

". . . nine, ten, eleven." That's right. I remember there were eleven codices. This is all, Father George."

FATHER GEORGE
(Opening the nearest one)

"As you can see, these are in Greek. All five of us are expert at reading and writing Greek. We can copy them accurately and exactly."

ADAM

"What about pens and ink? Do you need supplies?"

FATHER GEORGE

"No, Sir, each of my scholars carries fresh papyrus for ten codices, two pens, several vials of ink and cloths."

A scholar touches his pouch for Adam to see.

Adam shakes his head, with surprise and relief.

FATHER GEORGE

"Brothers, let us not waste time. Each of you take one codex at a time and copy everything in it, including marginal notes just as they are. If you have doubts about signs, letters or words, ask me."

All four scholars are busy copying codices studiously.

Father George and Adam are seen walking around and looking over the copyists. Then Adam leads Father George towards the courtyard.

EXT   THE COURTYARD

ADAM

"Father George, when you have finished copying these papyri, what happens next?"

FATHER GEORGE

"We will send them to our elders in Alexandria, Antioch and Rome. We will also send detailed notes about how these codices came into my possession. Of course, I will mention your name as the faithful grandson of Matthew the Disciple who wrote them. Then, devout scholars will critically examine these writings and determine whether they are worthy of acceptance by us. If accepted, these diaries will become part of our Holy Scriptures about our blessed Messiah."

ADAM

"Do you think they will be accepted?"

FATHER GEORGE

"Sir, I read parts while my scholars were copying. In my humble opinion these are genuine writings which are more than sixty or seventy years old. And you have witnessed that they were given to you by your grandpa who was a disciple of the Messiah. Therefore these diaries are worthy to be accepted by us. We already have two books which we call the Good News or Gospels. Your grandpa's diaries may become a third Gospel for us. But Sir, that may take a long, long time of debate and examination and meditation by our saints in Alexandria, Antioch and Rome."

ADAM

"Fantastic! I hope your effort will bear some useful fruit, Father George."

FATHER GEORGE

"Thank you, Sir. You have been very kind. I bless you with my whole heart. You are letting me copy them for the followers of your grandpa's Messiah. Actually, <u>we</u> are the body of The Messiah on earth. So, in a symbolic way, sir, these diaries are going to reach the Messiah, just as your grandpa intended, don't you think?"

ADAM

"You speak beautifully, Father George. In a way you may be correct. I like your conversation."

FATHER GEORGE

"Truthfully, we Christians venerate the memory of your grandpa as a disciple of Jesus our Messiah. If you demolish this house, your grandpa's diaries may be buried, or taken somewhere else and lost. Why don't you consider putting them into our custody? We will respect them as true originals—and your grandpa's name will be preserved with these diaries for all time."

ADAM

"Father George, you are a nice man. Let me think about it tonight."

EXT   NEXT DAY RIVER JORDAN STREET, (STREET FACING MATTHEW'S HOUSE)

Adam and Antonio are at the gate. They are waving farewell to Father George and his group who are already on the street.

Suddenly, Father George rushes towards Adam. He embraces Adam, places his crucifix on Adam's forehead.

FATHER GEORGE

"The Blessing of Almighty God and our Blessed Messiah be upon you, Sir. Once again I thank you for placing your grandpa's diaries in my humble hands. They will reach your grandpa's Messiah's devoted followers, just as your grandpa must have intended."

Father George and Adam embrace each other warmly. Adam appears to be moved. Father George wipes a tear from his right cheek.

Father George turns and slowly re-joins Varianus. The six of them turn around and walk away, with their donkeys following.

The End